The Sky is the Limit

by Meridith Hankenson Alexander

The Collection of Original Facebook Posts as Written Between February 19, 2016 and July 31, 2016 following Schuyler Arakawa's "accident" when she was struck by a random boulder while traveling in Colombia, South America

Dedications

To our amazing Global Family,

For your love, your prayers and your undying support,

To the many, MANY Angels along our path including the amazing Estrada family and Chris, Georgette and Alexis T

And of course all of Schuy's friends whose love and determination continues to hold her strong! I can't begin to name you all so let me just say you KNOW how much you mean to us and you know who you are! And for all of you who blessed us with Novenas and prayers! Thank you!

To the incredibly generous members of the Go-Fund-Me family and the angel donors from all sectors. You will never know just how much of a difference you made in our lives. It was profound!

To the wonderfully gentle and supportive members of the media who have helped to share our story and create such power and such hope…including Kera, Wendy, Tracy, Cedric, Jason, Andrés and John

To the amazingly, caring "behind the scenes" supporters at Yale University, Peter S, and my Exeter Class of '77 family

To all of you who have helped to contribute to our well-being in one amazing way or another including Forrest, Adam, Allie, Nancy, Faf, the Souza "team", Sebastian, Morgan (for holding down the fort), Laura B, Neil, Lauryn, Laura L; Steph, Julian and the entire Granada family, Santi, Mercy & Family, Paige, Millie, Raquel, Izzy, Maria, Brontë, Schmitty, Kathryn, Olivia L, Kara, Kaity, Alex & Taylor, Gabe, Katie, Rob & Sue, Abby K, Stephen B, Ricardo, Jorge, Desirée, Lori P, Mr. T & Corbett Prep, Dyane & Troy, the ladies at Belmora, Eric and the staff at the Florida Aquarium, Johnnie C, Dave S, Zubin, Hernan, Jeffrey and Michael, Ken & Kerri Courtright , Kim & Matthew (and friends) and of course our Scoutcrest, NTDT and Strive families, Cat,

*Charleen, Chantel, Nina and
Raul ...*

*To the INCREDIBLE doctors
lead by Dr. Ariza (Colombia)
and Dr. Bullock (USA), nurses
lead by the sweet Violet, our
Miami ICU family (from Leo,
Hazel, and Julio to Josie and
all who watched over Schuy like
their own daughter), our
ENTIRE (YES EVERY ONE OF
YOU!) Miami Rehab family
lead by Dr. Alvarez , our
Tampa Rehab team (Heather,
Maggie, Trudi and ALL of you
special people!) and medical
teams both in Colombia and in
the US, including the AMAZING
Air Ambulance Team that
transported her from Colombia
to Miami, the incredible staff at
Jackson Memorial Hospital,
Ryder Rehab Center and
Tampa General; Florida Brain*

5

& Spine; Our lovely case manager from Florida Blue— You are TRULY our heroes!

To the ever-nurturing, ever loving therapists (Dan, and Arleen) who have helped and continue to help Schuy sweet Schuy overcome this boulder... To the Sandras, Marc and the welcoming faces of TGH for your humor and smiles...

To our wonderful Colombian "family" who so generously took us in while Schuy was in Manuel Beltran and to the ABSOLUTELY HEROIC RAFTING COMPANY GUIDES who managed against all odds to get Schuyler to help and then who stayed by our side, fed us and even drove our luggage four hours to the plane--you are our Colombian angels;

To the Incomparable Dana, my "adopted daughter", there are no words..!

To Jordan and to Saya's amazing fiancé Robert, thank you for supporting our entire family during this challenge;

To Joe for enduring the onslaught of chaos and for breaking random hallway exit signs (i.e. for the unintentional fits of laughter)

And to my ever heroic family: my mom, my dad and Kathy, Jenny and the Halls, Frodo and Tinkerbell

To my angel on Earth, my "person", my new "sis", we absolutely would NOT be where we are today without you: the incredible "MAMA'LITA"

And of course to my phenomenal children Saya and Linden (Ryu) who absolutely exemplify the meaning of Greatness; I am truly the luckiest mom in the world! !

AND OF COURSE, LAST BUT NOT LEAST...

To my amazing "Peaceful Warrior Princess, the hero of many heroes in this story, to the amazing young woman who has already done so much to change this world but is showing unequivocally that she is not finished yet...

My beautiful SCHUYLER

... you truly do take our breath away

I love you!

CHAPTER 1

Greatness

Greatness... we hear about it on TV, in magazines, in social media... the athletes, the movie stars, the super models, the politicians... We worship it from afar... we live vicariously through it… we can almost taste it… we critique it.. we analyze it… we dissect it…

Until that one day when the phone rings and suddenly everything changes… when worlds collide and suddenly this thing called Greatness is thrust upon us — without warning — into our own quiet little world…

Suddenly, it's WE who have to come up with our own quivering version of Greatness… At this moment, like babes in the woods, we come face to face, silently and powerfully, with absolutely THE most vulnerable version of ourselves…

GREATNESS….

In spite of the fear… in spite of the sorrow… in spite of the pain…

In spite of the overwhelming desire to run, we have to find it…that elusive greatness…like the powerful refuge of the North star, we must embrace it as our only hope… in spite of the voice inside of our head that tells us that we can't… that we're not good enough… that we're not ready… that we're not worthy of such greatness….

On February 19th, 2016, I stood paralyzed in my kitchen, my hand still clutching that wretched phone. As of 3:15PM, nothing from the first 55 years of my life remained the same. I had just received a call from Colombia. It was my daughter's friend, Dana. Apparently, Schuyler, my youngest daughter, the baby of our family, while on a fellowship from Yale, had been crushed by a boulder just a few hours earlier and was not expected to survive. These things were not supposed to happen to "nice people"… to optimistic people… to those who were out there trying to "do good"….my two dogs looked at me emphatically, leashes still on. They knew that something was desperately wrong. They lay at my feet— dramatically quiet. I could barely move. I could barely breathe.

And certainly the last thing on my mind was the concept of Greatness.

And yet, this is not a tale of tragedy. This is the story of how against all odds, my two daughters, my son and I discovered something special... something that would move our lives forever... something that would catapult us far beyond the beaten path... something that would challenge us... something that would make us cry... and yet something that would lead us to a place of profound "knowing"....

In the midst of ventilators, medically induced comas and breathing tubes, we learned something profound about miracles... about hope... and about the "Impossible"

We discovered that greatness lies within each and every one of us. Greatness is not reserved for the rich, the famous or the select few.

Greatness is the moment when we realize that "the secret" of life lies far beyond the place where just being alive is good enough.

Greatness is far bigger than mere success. Greatness exists only when "successful" slips silently into the realm of impactful.

Greatness exists when we decide to pull ourselves up out of the dust to wear the cape of the Reluctant Hero …Greatness exists when we can go no further and yet we raise our head — fatigued and exhausted — to once again stand and rally…. to once again face those "insurmountable" challenges in Life, if that is what this thing called Greatness demands of us.

Greatness is finding our courage even in the midst of tragedy. Greatness is choosing to have faith even when the world tells us that there is no longer a valid reason to hope.

Greatness is not measured by dollar bills or gold medals or the number of followers that we have on our Twitter account.

Greatness is the unique fire that burns within each and every one of our souls that tells us that we CAN… it's a light that cannot be contained, captured or destroyed no matter how terrifying our circumstances.

Greatness is the common thread between each and every one of us that walks on this planet. Greatness is the spark that ignites the fire of universal hope.

Greatness flows through each and every one of our veins even when we cease to be able to breathe on our own.

Greatness can overcome the formidable, the impossible… Greatness can even overcome the catastrophic hit from a boulder.

Sky is the Limit is an accidental expression of inspiration. Yes, it's a story of my daughter and me—two otherwise "normal" albeit extremely optimistic human beings whose lives were changed forever in one moment by the strike of a boulder. When I originally wrote these posts just days after "the accident", I created them simply as updates— thinking that they would reach a few members of our friends and family. I was nervous… wondering if my optimism would be misconstrued as disrespectful… not the way that a mother should "act" under the circumstances.

And yet, something told me that I could not fall into despair. I could not portray my daughter as mortally wounded… because the moment that the world saw her as critically injured, that is what she was destined to become…

I braced for the potential criticism and dove into my first posts with a crazy determined optimism that seemed to be our only prayer…

So yes, what you will find in the following pages are my original posts lifted off our Schuy (pronounced Sky) is the Limit Facebook page… call it a mother's attempt to find Greatness in the midst of chaos and cataclysmic change. This is our story…

And yet, I hope that you will find that it's also the story of you — your own greatness, your own ability to win the race that can't be won, to find the treasure within yourself that those who don't believe in you would prefer to keep hidden…

These boulders that we face in our lives are not a lesson in how to face death. These boulders fall onto our paths so that we might finally learn the lesson of how to choose to live.

It's time…. time for you… time for us… time for everyone on this lovely planet to find their voice….

Their own unique greatness…

It's time for all of the passionate dreamers and believers, the enlightened warriors of optimism, to come together and to make our greatness heard.

The sky IS the limit… and sometime the limit is just the beginning…!

What follows are the actual Facebook postings from earlier days along this journey. Most of the posts were written by me. In a few cases, I have included updates by other key players in our story — angels, without whom I never would have found the strength to keep stepping.

A full book where I share more of my thoughts during this time and additional details will follow. In the meantime, I so hope that this can bring hope and light to your lives. Whether you are facing your own boulder or just working on unleashing your full greatness, know that we are all part of this amazing, vibrant global family — and we've got this! Here's to all of the GREATNESS that shines and shines and shines….

And so it began.....

CHAPTER 2

Boulder Impact

November 11, 2015 Schuyler (Approximately 3 months before the boulder strike)

Being raised by a single mom and grandmother, I've grown up knowing that women are real-life superheroes. The events happening around me, both here and back at home, have only confirmed that belief.

Part of my project in Peru is working with indigenous female weavers in rural communities to sell their products and provide them with an income. Because, statistically, when you help the women, you help the entire family. They work together, laughing and sharing conversations while they weave in order to create a better life for their families. These women walk over an hour and a half through the mountains to get to and from work, carrying their children and their supplies on their back.

To go to my other project in construction, I walk up 400 stairs in the middle of the mountains to build a preschool and, even after a month, I'm still winded every time. Today, I saw an

80 year-old woman carrying an entire bundle of bamboo on her back up the stairs. We stopped and asked her if she needed any help, but she said no as she smiled and moved us along.

On Monday, over 1000 Yale students came together to carry the weight of inclusivity and acceptance and to support the right for everyone to feel safe and loved on campus. My Yale experience wouldn't have been nearly as magical if I weren't surrounded by the beautiful women of color as I was. I am so incredibly proud of everyone that is helping to ensure that each person on campus has the right to feel that same magic and know that I am here with you in this push for growth.

To my mom, Meridith, and Gammy, Joyce, to the weavers who carry on this tradition, to that woman on the mountain, and to the women at Yale, and everywhere: Thank you for carrying the world upon your backs. Even from thousands of miles away, I hope you know that I'm always here to help carry the burden when the weight becomes too much.

February 19, 2016 / 4:49PM Meridith

Dear friends,

I am just learning that my dear sweet Schuyler has been in a critical accident in Colombia. I am of course going to fly down but if anyone has experienced anything like this and can share important insight/advice regarding international medical emergencies and potentially transporting a family member back to the states when stable, please private message me. Please send prayers. Our family so appreciates it!

February 20, 2016 (written by Schuyler's friend Dana from the organization that was to be Schuy's next leg in her fellowship Threads of Peru and who traveling with Schuy through Colombia at the time of the accident)

Friends family everyone and anyone,

My name is Dana, a close friend of Schuyler Arakawa and travel companion for what was to be our great Colombian adventure. I'm reaching out with the heaviest heart that Schuyler, as many have already seen, was in an extremely serious accident today and is currently in critical condition, fighting for her life.

While on a rafting excursion today, a very large rock fell from about 30 feet above where we were swimming, landing directly on Schuyler's head and causing a veritable laundry list of near fatal injuries. The most serious of which are grave fractures and trauma to the skull and face, lung damage and five fractured vertebrae in her spine. Its a God-given miracle not only that we were able to evacuate her to the nearest hospital quickly enough, but that she survived at all.

Schuyler underwent multiple surgeries this afternoon and although being monitored 24/7 overnight in the ICU, we have been told that until her condition stabilized in the coming days, we only have our prayers. I cannot express my gratitude that she has been attended to, and is being cared for, by a very capable medical staff and that they will keep us informed of any and all updates until we're able to be with her again in the hospital tomorrow morning. Her mother, Meridith Hankenson, and sister, Saya Arakawa, are already traveling from their home in Tampa, FL to Colombia.

This girl is the light of the world. In my life only since last October, from the moment she walked through my office door in Cusco, she captured my heart. Schuyler touches the lives of anyone she meets, smiling with her whole body and heart at friend, family and stranger. She knows no prejudice, no ill thoughts toward anyone. I have thought every day since meeting Schuyler that I could change the world by being 1/4 of the person that she is.

I beg you all to pray, send positive energy, share this message, do whatever you can or want to do for the world to join behind this incredible young woman. In 22 years spreading joy to all those around her, my heart can only accept that there is an entire lifetime ahead for her to continue painting the world in her technicolors.

With all my heart and love,

Dana

February 20, 2016 ·— Meridith

To our dear wonderful global family...I cannot begin to express the love and gratitude that we feel for all the love headed our way. I believe in the powerful miracle of Belief. I ask you all to see Schuyler Arakawa at her most joyous , most vibrant, most healthy and most alive. That is how I see her. That is the vision of herself that I intend to bring to her. The more of you who can help us hold that vision strong the more I know she will feel it. There can be no way but that she can return to that perfect state. Please believe and see her only in her greatness. I do. I do. Much love and so much humble appreciation for all of you!

February 20, 2016 ·— Meridith

Dear Schuy family!

Arrived! This is a glimpse of the magical land that brought Schuyler's Joie de vivre spirit to Colombia. As we make our way over the mountains to the hospital it struck me to ask anyone who might want to share a few words of inspiration with Schuyler Arakawa to please share them below. I will share each and every one of them with her to speed up her recovery. Love you all and thanks a million!!

February 20, 2016 ·— Dana

Every wish, hug, kiss, message of love, prayer or thought from around the world will be passed along to Schuyler in just a few short hours after being allowed back to the hospital. Our hope is to speak with the neurosurgeon that performed the most serious surgeries today as early as possible and will write with any updates when we can reconnect to Internet. Anyone and everyone can feel free to call me and please either leave a voicemail with your number to call back if I don't answer immediately or call back a little afterward. Schuyler can move mountains.

Let's give her everything we have to pull through. Much much much love, Dana

February 20, 2016 -Meridith

Hello dear friends. A humble request for help if you are so inclined ...Schuyler is still working her magic even from a coma. We have seen her. I won't kid you, there is a major road ahead-- from major head and eye trauma to major brain concerns. We are working to get her transported to bogota to stabilize her then hopefully on to Miami soon. Alexis has taken the initiative to create a fundraiser since the needs appear to be pretty massive. If you feel inclined in your heart to help at all, well there are not enough words to express. Any token of love and assistance would be appreciated.

This is the link to Schuyler's GoFund Me campaign:

https://funds.gofundme.com/mobile/dashboard?url=ztq2n4r8

Please share this with everyone you can. Much love and again thank you all for your love and support!

GoFundMe Dashboard

https://funds.gofundme.com/mobile/dashboard?url=ztq2n4r8

FUNDS.GOFUNDME.COM

February 21, 2016 ·— Dana

An update from Colombia for all those praying for our little girl,

Schuyler Arakawa is still stable but in delicate condition, needing to be monitored for at least another 24 hours at the hospital here in Socorro for her more serious injuries. But with her continued strength and mountain climbing perseverance, Schuyler is anticipated to be ready to travel back to Miami on

Monday morning with Meridith Hankenson and Saya Arakawa, both of whom arrived to us here today, to receive the best medical attention available at home.

This little songbird isn't out of danger yet, probably far from it, but we are surrounded by loving caring and capable people that have already shown us kindness unlike anything we could have ever imagined. Keep prayers and love flowing. Together we'll help Schuyler move this mountain and come back smiling to us ASAP.

Much much love and doing our best to keep updates coming to everyone.

Dana

February 21, 2016 ·Meridith

Good morning, dear global family! This is Schuyler's mom. First of all, may I say once again how humbled we all are by all of this generosity. This is truly a special moment in our lives as we celebrate the wonder of this special loved one's journey.

As we get ready to head over to the hospital, in the true spirit of all that our lovely Schuyler is about, this morning is a day to celebrate the heroes in this quest to propel Schuyler Arakawa's journey forward. We used to joke and call Schuyler "mini me" so let me tap into those parallel lines and imagine how she might want to craft this page if she were here to write this herself. My heart cries out, PLEASE, celebrate the heroes-- for there are more than you can believe.

Yes, there are challenges and we will face them, but out of this horror is more goodness than one could have ever wished for. So, dear wonderful friends and family, let me share with you some of the people that have been Schuyler's Columbian heroes....

Chapter 1: The family.... Ricardo and Luzangela

This amazing family live doors away from the hospital in this gloriously authentic home. It's a home filled with love and passion and the deep, richly tangible "joie de vivre" that Schuyler thrives on. One of the early buildings in Socorro, you enter the home and ascend into an enchanted "garden" home. I entered for the first time at night-- late night. I was captivated by the arches, the decor, the live plants, the wood... and then I looked up and KNEW that Schuyler had "brought" us here and must be smiling/giggling as she saw me "get it". The ceiling in the middle of the home was (yes) the SKY -- and a sky brimming with stars just the way that Schuyler loves it.... a few tears momentarily but an incredible warmth at the synchronicity of life.

I want to get to the hospital so I will save more of this musing for later, but know that even in her challenge, she continues to create magic! So, the faces.... the hero family who has taken us in like the most loving of Columbian parents.... with the UBER HERO DANA.... believe in the goodness of the human spirit. It is all around us even in the midst of this "tragedy". Gaze at the special family that has welcomed us with open arms and stayed all day with us at the hospital. Every moment not spent with Schuyler is spent scouring computers for information, communicating with other special heroes (more on them to come) from afar. Here, dear friends we start the celebration of this journey and all of the GREAT THINGS that it says about this tiny globe that we all call home and that sweet Schuy has loved beyond measure!!

Thank you and love you all! Meridith

February 21, 2016 ·Meridith

Dear Global Family and Friends....
(From Schuy's mom, Dana and Saya
Arakawa) The magic continues! The
power of your love and energy toward
Schuyler Arakawa is changing the world.
As part of our family now, let me share
with you the miracles that we have
discovered today because you will see
WITHOUT DOUBT that Schuyler was
reaching out not only to us, but to each
and every one of you that loves her so
profoundly.

First, the medical miracle: our first
news of the day was from the wonderful
general surgeon who has become such a
champion of our amazing Schuyler. He
said that he has never seen anything like
it and insisted on showing us the actual
footage of this morning's brain scan
compared to yesterday's scan. He
pointed out DRAMATIC changes in the
scan. Aside from the swelling going
down, there were improvements that
would have been celebrated A WEEK
FROM NOW. To see them only 24 hours

later are in his words literally "miraculous". Remember that Schuyler Arakawa is not out of the woods yet by any means, so this information brought tears…

So you can imagine, we went into the ICU feeling much hope. We had mentioned how I intended to take Schuyler's phone and play some of her song list for her since she so loved music. I noted that I would have preferred to play a John Mayer mix on Pandora, but alas we had no internet connection. That just wasn't possible. We would have to settle for her music library.

We moved to the ICU scrub station.This involves donning gowns, caps and scrubbing down then disinfecting. I (Meridith) did have my phone on me because it houses my credit cards. I wanted to keep those secure. Up goes my phone onto the top of the paper towel dispenser so that I could wash down. Friends, I kid you not, all of a sudden BLASTING out of my phone came Izzy's SOMEWHERE OVER THE RAINBOW--- and yes, I do not have that song in my music library.

We were stunned and there was a moment of confusion. I started asking how that had happened-- especially since it is a favorite song that Schuy and I connect with! I picked up my phone and there was the Pandora emblem in full view and SOMEWHERE OVER THE RAINBOW had just launched without the internet. In front of the Pandora emblem was the pop-up asking if I wanted to connect to the internet saying that there were two options: both password protected.

Needless to say, I burst into tears and headed over to Schuyler! Dana, Saya Arakawa and I held hands and teased Schuyler that she must have worked her magic to make this happen. We were in awe and not sure how this had happened but what followed soon elevated to a level where we just KNEW that each and every song was a form of communication from dear Schuyler as she lay there in her medically induced coma. She is known for her desire to communicate so she created a song list so beautiful and so poignant that we wish to share it with you.

Below I share the song list with a couple of notes pulled from the moments that made those songs so relevant. We would love for those of you who wish to concentrate energy toward this remarkable soul to play this song list in support of Schuyler. As you listen, see her with that huge smile, arms thrown wide embracing the moment. We love you all and thank you beyond measure for all of your love and support!

Behold, Schuyler Arakawa's song list, her gift to us all:

- Israel Kamakawiwiole - Somewhere Over The Rainbow/What a BeautifulWorld

- Christian Perri - A Thousand Years

- Train - Hey Soul Sister (a Song that She and Saya Arakawa consider "their" own)

- Coldplay - The Scientist

- Jack Johnson - Do you Remember

- John Mayer - Say

- Ben Rector - When A Heart Breaks

- The Goo Goo Dolls - Slide (Schuyler moved almost like she was doing a body roll - AMAZING!)

- Parachute - She is Love (A powerful moment since only Schuyler knew that this is a song that Saya Arakawa wants to have played when she walks down the aisle)

- Peter Hollens - I Won't Give up

- Mick McAuley & Winifred Horan - To Make You Feel

- Coldplay - Fix You

- Passenger - Things You've Never Done…

- American Authors - Best Day of My Life (This blew us away. This song came on immediately following a visit from the anesthesiologist who remarked to us that we have many reasons to believe that not only will Schuyler live, but he expects her to continue improving and recovering)

- Sam Smith - Stay With Me (as we began to pray together with Schuyler)

- Jasmine Thompson - Titanium (Particularly significant since this is the second time that song has played. As Saya and I were being driven yesterday through hours of mountainous terrain, the van's radio played nothing but South American music. I got a call from Dana with an update on Schuy in which she mentioned that Schuyler had moved her feet when Dana had mentioned my mother Joyce Hall and I. Saya and I were overjoyed and began expressing hope. All of a sudden, Titanium popped onto this station of totally Spanish music. Never again in that entire 3 hour trip did we hear a western song.)

- A Fine Frenzy - Almost Lover (when we told Schuyler we were going to leave for a bit but would be back soon to visit, this song filled with lyrics that say "goodbye" closed "the show".)

So, yes, more on the heroes is yet to come including THE AMAZING RAFTING TEAM that defied all odds to get Schuyler Arakawa to the hospital and the phenomenal doctors that performed miracles by giving her this chance to survive....! But for now, please accept what we are sure is a gift from Schuyler Arakawa: this song list. Please play it loud and strong in support of our dream girl! Many thanks to you all!

February 21, 2016 · New Haven, CT · Katie Galbraith on Schuyler's FB page

DUDE. check you out!! This is what popped up when Allie Souza started typing your name in on Facebook. Look how many people you have inspired!! Over 48,000!??!! You are incredible and you are nothing short of amazing. Love you to infinity and beyond my babe. Keep fighting and know you've got the world in your corner. xxxxxxxx

February 21, 2016 —Amalita

Schuyler has been placed in a beautiful "cocoon" by all prayers energy good wishes --- all protecting her and calling for a chance to live! Her beautiful soul - person- spirit is healing within this "cocoon" - Schuyler keep feeling all of our love!

Hello All,

Today is the day we will be trying to bring our girl home!!!

I just want to thank everyone so much for the outpouring of love and prayers that Schuyler Arakawa has received over the past three days. It has been incredible to witness just how many people Schuyler has touched in her 22 amazing years-- You've already made such a difference in this world Sky Baby and I look forward to many, many more years of your incredible light!!!!

There are many moving parts to today's success so please pray for the most seamless of transitions from Colombia to America. Schuyler's stability during the many hours of traveling is of the utmost importance. While she has shown incredible improvement, she is by no means out of the woods and will need every positive thought and prayer to protect her.

Thank you to all those who have done everything in their power to try to guarantee today's continued success. Dr. Javier Ariza and his incredible team of doctors and nurses at the hospital have done everything in their power to keep our girl healing and stable. Mrs. Amalita Salazar- Estrada you are Schuyler's Angel and we thank you for being our Colombian connection throughout all of this. Lastly, many prayers to Schuyler's Mom, Meridith, sister Saya and dear friend Dana who have all been by Schuyler's side and will be traveling back to Miami as well today. You are so loved.

Please stay strong. ❤ ❤ ❤

As we all know, the SCHUY is the limit when it comes to this girl! Please send Prayers and Love!!!

https://www.gofundme.com/ztq2n4r8/share/gfm/fb_d_5_q

Good morning, dear global family and friends! It's Meridith (Schuyler Arakawa's mom).

Saya Arakawa and I are finishing up our wonderful breakfast courtesy of our new Columbian host family: fresh fruit, warm bread and cafe con leche. Not much time for length here, but I definitely want to echo our awe and appreciation for this tsunami of love and support!

Today is THE day! We will be flying our dear Schuyler (thanks to all of your help) to the welcoming arms of the amazing doctors of University of Miami.

A couple of focus points for those of you who have been so instrumental in giving dear Schuyler such power and momentum.

Today will particularly focus on the challenge of her eyes. We have some of the best doctors in the world ready to examine and assess the challenges that lie ahead regarding her vision. Please send your energy and your prayers specifically to her sight today. We ask that you envision her strong and at her best.

We have yet to get the morning update, but last night was cause for continued celebration... delicious wiggles of her toes, flutters of her shoulders, a squeeze of her hand. She is still definitely in a coma but we can feel the energy for sure!

For those of you who want to reach out to Schuyler Arakawa, we suggest (and invite you) to post Youtube songs, mp3s, written verse, shoutouts, love poems, audio books, favorite quotes, anything that will make a heart soar... in other words "audio flowers" until we get those eyes bright again!

We will be back to you with an update shortly, but for now we run to get the gorgeous sweet one ready for the next step in this magnificent journey toward renewed health!

Good bye Columbia for now! We couldn't be more grateful to all of those here in this amazing country who have opened their hearts and their homes to our darling girl and to us. To the river guides (more on them soon) who fought all odds to get her off the river and to the hospital, you are our heroes! We love you! To the doctors and medical team of Manuel Beltran (Socorro)-- there are no words. You will be part of Schuyler Arakawa's heart beat for eternity. Good bye Columbia! Hello new world!

Much love!!

Meridith

February 22, 2016 · Meridith

Home to Miami!! Touch down approximately 6pm!

Oh my... God is good - things are all happening and our global angel is on way home!

Air ambulance in route and on course.

Terrestrial ambulance in route and on course- will arrive airport (Bucaramanga)around 4:30 - in perfect time to arrive and transport to air ambulance - our Global angel is stable and going along with her journey !

God continue to bless!

Global family- as Meridith has expressed-

Here is straight from Meridith's txt...

"We can see the airport on top of the mountain ahead!"

Air ambulance has arrived Bucaramanga - our global angel is in Bucaramanga and very close to arriving airport!

February 22, 2016 (Amalita)

Hi global family-

Have been informed by terrestrial ambulance - they are transferring Schuyler at this very second to air ambulance!

God is good! Amazing is a better way to express ! Keep praying and sending good vibes!

February 22, 2016 (Amalita)

One step closer Schuyler !!!! You have made it so far ! Your strength is to be admired!!!!! Know that your global family is sending many prayers and strength your way!

February 22, 2016 (Amalita)

Global family-Schuyler has boarded her air ambulance!!!!!!!!!

February 22, 2016 (Amalita)

Global family- Here she comes!!!

Words from Meridith's txt..,

"Ready for take off! Off we go!!

Taxiing away! Like this team. Tia, Kristina and Guillermo. See you soon!"

They are in route!!!!"

February 22, 2016 (Amalita)

To this most amazing global family-

Our global angel with her most miraculous mother and sister are in close proximity above - flying USA skies! Ambulance to transport from Miami international to hospital will be ready to transport once plane lands.

"Schuyler - your strong and beautiful spirit has not stopped shinning!

February 22, 2016 (Amalita)

Our global angel has landed!!!! Now they prep to transfer to ambulance then off to hospital!!!

February 22, 2016 (Alexis)

SCHUYLER HAS LANDED IN MIAMI!!! ❤ ❤

God is so good! Welcome home sweet Sky!!! We love you so much!!

Everyone please continue praying for round two of Schuyler's hospitalization and healing! We have a long way to go but she is finally home!!

#TheSchuyisTheLimit

February 22, 2016 (Amalita)

To all of whom have joined Schuyler in prayer - good wishes- sending your energy and love - as Meridith has referred to us all - the global family:

I would like to share Chris' message sent to Dr. Javier Ariza - head Doctor of the ICU unit at the regional Hospital Manuel Beltran , whom led - along with other amazing specialists and nurses : the same battle as Schuyler : a fight for her to live! Our global angel is alive! And now back in USA fighting for a continuous recovery – keep your prayers my friends to continue surrounding her with our support!

Chris' message:

"Dr. Ariza she is in the ICU at University of Miami Jackson Memorial Hospital. Thank you. Thank you!!!!"

God Bless our Colombian doctors whom saved our global angel: Schuyler Arakawa!`

Welcome home

CHAPTER 3

The Angel Has Landed

February 23, 2016 **(Amalita)**

GLOBAL FAMILY:

Thank you for all of your prayers, thoughts, good wishes and vibes that have surrounded and continue to surround our global angel Schuyler.

Some of you may be wondering how she is:

Granted the permission from Meridith to share - she asks all you - global family - to keep your hearts strong for our little warrior girl. She wants you to know that she's in stable condition, being well cared for. Meridith is receiving helpful and direct information from her doctors. She asks for your continued prayers and good vibes as we all patiently wait for each minute, hour and day to continue within the process of her recovery with no time frame to be sure.

"keep your hearts strong for our little warrior girl"

February 23, 2016 Meridith

Greetings, dear Global Family!!! This is Schuyler Arakawa's mom! First of all, I want to thank everyone SO SO much for all of your amazing blasts of energy that you have been sending our way! The prayers, the warm wishes, the hugs (both tangible and intangible), the generosity... SO MUCH MORE than I could have every wished for..... please let me launch this post by saying that I feel as if I am being cradle by no less than God Himself. In the midst of this heartache, I am seeing Heaven on Earth because Schuyler Arakawa, my family and I are being surrounded literally by angels. Who could ask for more? You are showing me a goodness in people, a goodness in mankind and a goodness in this planet that I "believed" in, but now am SEEING.

[Sidenote: one of Schuy and my favorite sayings has always been believing is seeing but I realize now that those had been merely beautiful words. As of Friday, this has become my reality because YOU dear friends have made this SO.]

As you suspect, my life has been a whirlwind---well, quite honestly more like a tsunami--since Friday, but particularly over the past few days while we work on getting Schuyler here to Miami. I confess that I have not been able to even glance at this wonderful page. Between lack of internet while in the hospital in Columbia and a battery in my phone that always seemed to die too quickly, I apologize for being more incommunicado than I would have liked.

Regarding the generosity on the funding page, I confess that I hadn't had a moment to even look at the page. I have yet to visit it. Sooooo, let me just say that when someone just a few moments ago told me the amount and some of the offers, well, I was humbled to tears!!! I CANNOT BEGIN TO EXPRESS the appreciation, gratitude, relief, hope--- the MYRIAD of emotions that this has brought to me and to our entire family. THANK YOU, THANK YOU, THANK YOU, THANK YOU!!! I could not possibly express what these gifts mean to us!

So, our darling Schuyler Arakawa.... yesterday was quite the trek. If you don't know Colombia, imagine mountains--- and then multiply the height by about a thousand. I have lived in the Rockies and I was STUNNED by these mountains. Absolutely the ONLY way to get Schuyler to the air ambulance was to subject her to almost 4 hours of travel through these winding environmental feats of nature. Two treacherous lanes with heavy traffic being traveled at highway speed with the ground ambulance weaving around the other vehicles even with a no-visibility turn straight ahead....! Saya and I were crammed next to each other in the front seat next to the driver. Let's just say it was an adventure...

[Insert: next post will focus on the amazing Colombian heroes that I want to recognize. However, I cannot mention leaving Colombia without asking everyone to send their MAJOR thanks to entire Colombia Rafting Expidiciones team who literally not only saved Schuyler's life and got her to the hospital, but they stayed with us literally THE ENTIRE DAY each day at the hospital and even drove the entire 3 1/2 - 4 hour trip to the airport simply to transport our luggage so that both Saya and I could travel in the ambulance! They bought us food before we embarked on the plane and even after we had said our good-byes, they waited inside for an additional 30 minutes to make sure that our flight did take off!}

The plane!!! Schuyler Arakawa, Saya and I were met by one of the most beautiful sights EVER: the long awaited air ambulance with an amazing team that whisked Schuy effortlessly and beautifully to the Miami airport.

So here we finally are... home soil... creme de la creme environment... the best of the best team!

Update on her progress:

Schuyler Arakawa has already begun impressing the team with her progress. There are still some grave concerns that will be immediately addressed. As you might guess, since she is still in the ICU, visitors are of course not allowed. They are going to be tackling some of the major threats to her survival/well being within the next week. They still have her heavily sedated but the team has been relaying some great reasons for hope and progress. We will share some of those as we move further along and know that they are permanent.

Schuyler has been blasting through hurdles at a speed that even the Miami team has been impressed with. We ask you to please continue your prayers and strong energy! Please continue to see her at her best and most vibrant. Please continue to share your words, your songs and "verbal flowers" for her. They will be INTEGRAL in her healing process.

Moving forward:

We have so many new, wonderful friends that are expressing their love and concern for dear Schuyler Arakawa, that we have an idea. We are going to launch a foundation called (what else) "The Schuy's the Limit" and create a public facebook page. Initially, this will be a public page to learn more about this wonderful spirit and to celebrate this powerful journey that she is embracing.

Eventually, as she conquers these battles and moves back to her deliciously happy place, it will be a foundation to empower others. As you know, social enterprise and empowering others has been a major passion (and gift) for Schuyler Arakawa. We will be moving these updates more toward that page so that our global family can continue to expand and nurture. We will update you shortly with that page info.

Schuy has many intense battles ahead of her but our sweet wonderful Schuyler, as you all know, is the stuff that great adventures and fairy tales are made of! Eventually, I will have a moment to begin to read some of these amazing posts and to see some of the amazing gifts and offers of help that we have been receiving. If I have not thanked you personally, please KNOW that I appreciate every word, every gesture, every thought, every tangible gift and contribution!! I truly have been so engrossed in this journey that I haven't had a chance to really see the specifics.

On behalf of Ryu, Saya, myself and OF COURSE on behalf of Schuyler, we thank you from the bottom of our hearts. You have given us the gift of humanity-- the gift of seeing human goodness in its most glorious sense.

The following updates all come from Schuys the limit page from Meridith

February 25, 2016

I am still so humbled and amazed by all of the love and support that Schuyler Arakawa and our family are receiving! For those of you have donated to her treatment, there are no words to properly express our appreciation!

In order to better embrace our new global family, we have created the following public page where you all can share your love, prayers and support. Know that we love you all, that we are inspired by you all and that the best "show of support" for Schuyler Arakawa on this day of her first surgery is to carry this bright light of kindness with you everywhere you go today. Please share your love, your warmth, you generosity with all whom you encounter today in honor of our dear Schuy's lovely spirit.

"You is smart.

You is kind.

You is important."

One of Schuy's favorite quotes!

February 25, 2016

Wow! I am speechless! More than 1000 likes in less than 12 hours? I am beyond moved! Thank you more than you can imagine!

February 25, 2016

We LOVE all the support from all the people around the world and need your prayers. We believe this page will allow us to share updates without transforming her personal page into something that she will not recognize when she gets better.

This page is to continue building strength for Schuyler through prayers, stories, pictures, videos, music and pure love - any form of sonic flowers that your heart desires.

February 25, 2016

Today is a transformative day as Schuyler embarks on the adventure of her first surgery, being tended to by the most capable medical professionals imaginable (THANK YOU WORLD!)!

She is stronger in mind and spirit than ever before. The miracles continue, the progress continues and we can tell you with absolute certainty that Schuyler is 1,000% in this fight.

We ask for your prayers, positive energy and love from afar as we take this first step in Schuyler's beautiful journey back to health and wholeness.

February 25, 2016

While resting the night before the accident, this is one of the songs that

Schuyler was listening to. Also warrants mentioning that she was staying in a yurt that night - true Schuyler fashion to find the coolest imaginable hostel in the Colombian mountains!

Dispatch - "Bound By Love" [Official Lyric Video]

http://www.facebook.com/dispatch

Little Schuyler is in surgery and in wonderful, loving hands! Keep prayers soaring and listen along with us to her fighter song. Schuyler, you know no weakness and we're all here with you!

Miracles galore from our radiant girl! Schuyler came through surgery in mere hours, sending our hearts soaring with happiness. We KNOW that it is because of the continued flood of love, support and prayers from our global family. Schuyler knows that you are with her and your strength is making her stronger!

February 26, 2016

Dear Amazing Global Family and Friends!

This is Schuy's mom. What an amazing few days! It's hard to express the deluge of emotions one feels when one hears the doctors use the word "success" when referring to the critical spine fracture procedure that Schuyler underwent yesterday. More miracles...!

Many of you have asked me how I am holding it all together through this. As I expressed to some of my friends, this experience is more powerful than I could have ever imagined. It's a terrifying yet almost religious experience. The new friends... the new "family"... the love... the generosity... the unfolding of so many new perspectives...

I'm actually gripped with a strangely focused almost "peaceful warrior" presence. I have no doubt--- no fear-- no sorrow --- nothing but all engulfing belief. The skies are bigger, brighter, more filled with stars. There is no wavering-- only a profound "knowing" that all will be well. Yes, I have seen nightmares, but those pale in the presence of a world of sublime grace. To feel the prayers, the hope, the generosity of friends, families and "strangers" is to feel the breath of a choir of angels on my face. The world's outpouring of love and generosity has changed my world in a way that no "mere" brush with death can compete.

We are strong through this not because we fight to be strong but because the "knowing" is so strong-- the faith is so strong-- that it is "natural" to be strong. We feel your prayers. We feel your hope. With your wind at my back I face this quest with the determination of a warrior and the faith of a saint. I never feel that I walk alone and I will never falter.

I love life. I believe in life. I love this planet and I love my children as if this love was the very oxygen that feeds my body.

Our dear Schuyler still has a long way to go in this healing process but thanks to your love and prayers, miracles seem to be a daily occurrence. One intense procedure along our path is behind us with several critical procedures still ahead. The challenges both physical and psychological are intense. For now, her body must rest and recoup. We ask that you continue to pray for our sweet warrior child. A critical (and long) procedure will take place on March 7. Until then, we will nurture this beautiful girl and beautiful spirit and help to fortify her along this journey.

We love her. We believe in her and with your love and support, we KNOW that this story will have a rich and beautiful "ending". On behalf of our ever vibrant and awe-inspiring "dream child", we thank you. Life is a mere century. Savor it. Taste it but most importantly live it as if the "Schuy is the Limit".

Much love and appreciation!

Meridith

February 29, 2016

Hello, dear beautiful global family and friends! What a magnificent day it is proving to be here in Miami! It's a leap day in a leap year so what better way to celebrate than with leaps and bounds forward for our lovely Schuy!

For me, I woke up bubbling nervousness, purpose and the chills of the pending "yet-to-come". It's a strange place to be these days-- familiar in the sense that it's still me, but unfamiliar in that I know that the world will never be the same. I feel a huge sense of "enormity". Any sense of control that might have pretended to live inside of me on the Thursday before the accident has been replaced with the awe of greater meaning and the need to remain comfortable in the midst of such a wave of momentous change.

Your prayers and beautiful healing vibes are definitely working! They are awe-inspiring and important. The miracles are as much yours as they are ours! Yes, dear friends, it is official: the doctors have confirmed that when they open her eyes, SHE CAN SEE FROM BOTH EYES. We absolutely KNOW that the day will come when she will open those beautiful eyes on her own and gaze with such happiness out onto this amazing planet! Doctors were cheering! I was cheering! Even Schuy was wiggling her toes. This dear powerhouse is fighting on all cylinders for sure so we invite you to give a little whoop whoop of appreciation to the Universe when you can! We are ALL IN this momentum and with your continued love & support, this is unstoppable!

But being that it's such a special day, Schuyler wasn't about to stop at simply one miracle. Wink! You can practically touch her desire— it's that palpable! Her progress is so pronounced that the respiratory therapists decided to see if she can (yes) begin to breathe on her own…. after a bit of initial coughing and adrenalin rushes, they were finally able to turn the ventilator down and allow her to basically breathe on her own with just a little bit of help from the machine!!! There are still plans to give her a tracheostomy tomorrow (so more prayers please) but we are definitely headed in the right direction!

But why stop there? Progress has been so remarkable that the neurological team has bumped up the date of the major head surgery to this Friday! The rest of the week for Schuyler will be spent in recuperative sleep where her body can continue to fortify and build up strength for this next procedure.

We ask that you continue to pray and send us those healing vibes. Many of you know that Schuyler's middle name is Sachi (meaning happiness in Japanese) so if you want to build up mountains of

"Schuylerian" energy for our girl, we ask that you spend these next 7 days laughing, dancing for "no reason", living, loving, savoring, basking…! Hug a random stranger who needs a lift! Sing out loud! Spread your kindness like candy! Dig deep and be every little bit of greatness that you can be! Life is large. Life is sweet! Angels are everywhere including within. We are meant to be here and life is meant to be fun!

We love you all so much and thank you beyond words for all the beauty and joy that each and every one of you sends! From our hearts to yours: Schuy's the Limit!

Much love,

Meridith
(Schuyler's mom)

Here's to our magical warrior "child" (thank you Kathryn Burns): https://www.youtube.com/watch?v=HOMMnQUu8C0

CHAPTER 4

Marching Fourth

March 4, 2016

Hello dear beautiful global family and friends! It's Schuyler's mom.

THE PROCEDURE HAS BEGUN! It is hard to capture what I am feeling other than an overwhelming sense of awe and purpose. The team of doctors here are amazing—a combination of young, vibrant youth and older seasoned "wise ones". The electricity and respect among the team members is tangible. Had Schuyler not been lying in bed in the middle of an ocean of tubes and monitors, one could look down from above and believe that one was in the center of a huddle of athletic champions….poised, eager, ready… totally engaged in the challenge of all that is about to unfold.

Schuyler looks radiant and ready. Like a tiny, fragile China doll— so superficially broken — but spiritually so phenomenally whole. Tubes and monitors are everywhere but there still is a calm energy…an elusive beauty to the confidence and all-embracing "potential" that floats in the air. Totally engulfed in the moment, we all know without saying that we are all part of something immensely reverent and powerful. THIS MOMENT is pure, enfettered LIFE.

Schuyler is indeed a miracle! Every doctor that we encounter has said that her spirit has defied all odds. She IS the ultimate peaceful warrior and even without the ability to communicate verbally, she inspires those around her. It is gripping to see the special bond within the ICU. I suppose none of us ever know (or quite honestly want to know) how we will react if we find ourselves in this situation. I can tell you that I certainly never in a million years thought when I last spoke with Schuy the day before her accident that my life (and hers) would change forever barely twelve hours later.

Surprisingly, there is more peace than panic. There is a "knowing" not simply a "belief" that all will be well. There is a huge sense of forgiveness…. forgiving the world for all of the "hard" life events that I have lived in the past… forgiving the rock for having fallen on my beautiful child… forgiving myself for past "shortcomings" that now have become unique strengths…. There is also an overwhelming sense of gratitude…. of course gratitude that Schuyler was blessed with survival and surrounded with amazing souls (and angels) who have made and who continue to make her survival possible… but also gratitude for the wisdom of Life, God, Eternity… and gratitude for the human spirit that contains more magic and power than we can ever fully identify or imagine.

Today, as Schuyler is gifted with 12 hours of surgery — surrounded by such medical genius and intent— I would humbly ask that you all tap into her natural ability to love and appreciate. Make today a day of sublime gratitude. Take a moment in Schuy's honor to stretch your arms out wide and embrace the horizon. Breathe in oceans of oxygen. Close your eyes and feeeeeeeeeel the pulse of our amazing planet. Laugh. Dance. Run. Cheer! Life is beyond amazing! We are meant to be here, each with our own amazing quirky gifts and unique "limitations"— the ultimate puzzle where each individual piece relies on the other crazy shapes to create the complete beautiful image. You are part of this special creation. You are strong and brilliant and vital— and you are one of the angels that are giving Schuyler and each of us in her family so many wings to rest our hearts on.

Today is a special day! The Schuy is the Limit!! Our hearts are mighty!

Much love,

Meridith

March 4, 2016

FIRST UPDATE: SCHUYLER IS STABLE AND DOING WELL! We have got this, world!!

March 4, 2016

Update: the neurological portion of Schuyler's surgery went well in spite of the surgeons discovering that the damage to her skull was even more pronounced than expected...

March 4, 2016

My dear darling global family and friends! Schuyler is OUT OF SURGERY AND THE SURGEONS BELIEVE THAT THE PROCEDURE HAS BEEN A TOTAL SUCCESS! Details will follow but for now, our family wishes you the sweetest of dreams and sends you the warmest of hugs! Feel the delicious texture of the sheets as you crawl into bed and know that Schuyler's warrior spirit is riding strong!!!! Much love!! Sweet dreams, all!

We could not be more grateful for all of your prayers!! Schuy IS the limit! CELEBRATE!!!

March 7, 2016

Hello dear glorious global family and friends! It's Schuyler's mom again!

More whirlwinds! More magic! First, a very special and exciting update: THE LAST OF SCHUYLER'S MAJOR PROCEDURES HAS NOW BEEN SCHEDULED FOR TOMORROW! For those of you early risers, please send out your most effervescent flood of prayers to our gentle spirit warrior. Tomorrow, it is all about healing Schuyler's precious legs.

Dear sweet Schuy is going to continue her titanium transformation beginning at about 6am tomorrow morning. She will have a rod placed in her right thigh then screws and wires in her left ankle, shin and knee cap. The miracles of modern science!

The swelling from Friday's huge brain and facial procedure continues to go down. Her lungs get stronger every day. Contrary to two weeks ago, doctors even have high hopes for her eyes! Yes, dear friends, our sweet Schuyler IS beating all odds and creating daily miracles.

She is still heavily sedated of course and on strong, strong pain meds but we feel the pulse of her energy and the peaceful breath of hope from the moment that we walk into her room. We are surrounded by this amazing team of doctors and nurses who have taken us under their wing. One of the nurses heard that I slept on the floor of Schuyler's room on Friday (on blankets with my pillow) and within an hour had moved us to a larger room with a chair that reclines. No surprise was to discover that this room has windows on two sides including windows that face (Schuyler would love it) the Miami sunset.

Speaking of magic, life always seems to find a way to take our breath away and to make us smile in the midst of nerves and tension. Today started out feeling like it might just be "one of those days".… from having my email account hacked at the hospital to potentially having someone walk off with not only my purse but my car keys, I felt just a little "off sync" for most of the day. A little bit more fragile… a little less centered.…

The day was drawing to a close and still no sign of my missing purse or my car keys. Not only did my car contain my suitcase with clothes but the thought that someone might be wandering the property with the ability to actually drive "the green hornet" inspired us to action. A tow truck was called only to arrive an hour later without the tools to pop open my car. As fate would have it though, this driver knew a lock company that could not only pop open my car but create an entirely new key on site. How glorious!

As we sat waiting for this dear man to arrive at the hospital, my daughter Saya suddenly remembered that the missing purse might actually be in the bathroom where we had stayed the night prior. The locksmith was already en route and Saya was ten minutes from the apartment so the plan was to see if our driver would wait to see if Saya's hunch was correct. When Saya was still about 5 minutes away, the driver arrived and happily agreed to wait.

He asked if I was a nurse and I told him no. I started sharing just a little bit about Schuyler. He immediately told me to expect a miracle. He said that he could see that we would see a miracle. He told me to remember this conversation and that especially on March 24, we would see a miracle. The conversation became increasingly more spiritual as Saya's fiancé came to check on me. He talked about a strengthening heart and mind. Before we knew it, this wonderful man was offering us his phone number in case he could help us while we were here. At that point, Saya called and my purse and keys had indeed been found. As I thanked this uplifting man and gave him a tip for his troubles, I of course asked his name. Robert and my jaws both dropped when he smiled and said "Heim" which means LIFE!

Like that crazy kaleidoscope web of destiny, all of a sudden it felt like the entire day had been leading us toward this moment when LIFE not only assured us that all was well but that SACHI / HAPPINESS (Schuy's middle name that translates to "happiness" in Japanese) would be restored to full force by the miraculous coming together of the energy of many.

Sound like a screenplay?!!

And so dear ones as I tuck myself into bed for a few hours of sleep, I share with you joy, hope, optimism and the ability of LIFE to surprise and delight you even in moments of intense stress. LIFE can be found where you least expect and in the people who might otherwise disappear into the crowd. Be open. Be calm. Be playful and expect miracles to occur even in the midst of "one of those days". We are ever evolving works of human art. Each moment is a fresh canvas. Dive into the paint. Get messy and (as Schuyler would urge) even paint outside the lines. We are unique and glorious human beings and the very next moment is the frame for a monumental now. Live, love and dream in masterpieces! Bask in the energy! The Schuy is the Limit!

Oh the miracles that tomorrow will bring! Thanks beyond words for your generosity, thoughts and prayers! Sweet dreams!!!

CHAPTER 5

ICU Sunshine Girl

March 7, 2016

Quick update to our wonderful glorious global family! Schuyler's team took time to grab one quick CAT scan before proceeding with the leg surgery. New start time: approximately 12:45pm so please keep those prayers and thoughts coming. She is wiggling her toes and ready to dance through this one last procedure! Schuy is the Limit for this Sunshine Girl (thank you Alexis!)

Super hugs!!! THANK YOU!! Love, Meridith, Schuy and everyone in this giant circle of love family!

March 9,2016

Hello dear wonderful global family and friends! It's Schuyler's mom again.

So Monday was quite the day, although not the day that we thought that we were anticipating...! Schuyler's leg surgery was ultimately postponed (until when, we don't yet know) due to some incoming emergencies and some hospital logistics. Yes, quite a sigh to know that Schuyler's condition is no longer considered the most potentially life threatening in the mix! We will let you know the moment that we hear about the rescheduled date, however, Monday may not have been surgery but it was beyond powerful...

There is the tendency to see and then believe. Our science and technology is amazing and therefore I think that it's fair to say that we place a huge value on "reality"/ logic /proven fact and statistics. That said, in spite of all the modern medicine that currently surrounds us here in Miami, Monday became a lesson in "impossibilities" and "I'm POSSIBILITIES". Dear friends, our mission here is not to defy reality or prove anything. Our focus is all about our "baby" Schuyler and yet Life keeps gracing us with profound learning and fairy dust.

There were four surgeons last Friday who tackled the job of "fixing" the damage to Schuyler's brain (prior to passing the torch to the maxillofacial team). On Monday, an ordinary moment became extraordinary when talking to two of the men on that team. One of these men has become a regular point person. He is not only adept at his craft, but we can tell that he has become emotionally invested in our sweet Schuy. On Monday, he shared with me that he has done probably 600 or more procedures for trauma to the brain. Virtually never had he seen such damage to the surrounding skull with virtually zero damage to the brain itself. He described the skull bone as having been so crushed that the slivers looked like bits of corn flakes. He was stunned that she had survived.

We keep hearing that same message over and over yet the immensity of this miracle was perhaps best captured by the second member of the team. He stood staring at Schuy from the foot of her bed and said that he just can't help but share how absolutely amazing it is to see her on the road to recovery. He went on to explain that the type of injury that dear sweet Schuy had to her lungs virtually always results in the loss of life on the scene prior to even making it to the hospital. The fact that Schuyler not only made it to the hospital but survived for an hour over unpaved roads is absolutely unbelievable — and that was just one of her wounds.

He went on to marvel that with as many broken bones as she had, her arteries managed to remain unscathed. Had they been even nicked, she could have (once again) died at the scene. Her back bone was of course also fractured and not protected until she got all the way to Miami. The fact that her spinal cord appears to be fine is impossible to comprehend. He went on to say that the brain's condition also defies logic. Looking at the amount of damage to the skull, it's hard to imagine that she could have survived that— much less that the brain itself appears to have sustained minimal damage.

This doctor finished by hugging me and saying that he has seen some great things but that Schuyler truly is a collection of miracles! She survives "in spite" of logic/reality. Her "I'm possible" perspective has redefined the boundaries between life and death in this case.

So tomorrow (or should I say later today) as you look out onto the beautiful sunshine and the breathtaking skyline, take a moment to let your mind wander. Today is the day to promise yourself that going forward, you will now "risk" believing in miracles. You will believe before you see. You will replace the "impossibilities" in your world with a treasure chest of "I'm possibilities"! Schuyler is 100% proof that miracles DO HAPPEN. And for that matter, MANY MANY MIRACLES can and do happen.

Expect greatness. Dream it. Feel it. Smell it. Touch it. Celebrate it long before reality unveils it. Life is a poetic balance of the real and the magical so explore every inch of your masterpiece's canvas!

Now, as I revel in the twists and turns of this journey, I must try to lull myself to sleep. Thank you for your continued prayers and support! Wishing you "evidence" of your own special miracle at every turn today! Be joyful. Live bold! The Schuy is the Limit!!!

Much love,

Meridith (Schuyler's Mom)

March 11, 2016

Hello dear beautiful global family! It's Schuyler's mom.

Tonight I sit in this lovely Miami apartment captivated by the brilliance of the moment. As fate would have it, the "friend of a friend's apartment" sits atop the 37th floor and one side gazes upon the ocean and upon the other a kaleidoscope of twinkling city lights.

The power of the human metaphor is breathtaking. The ebbs and flow of the Universe can sometimes feel like the mighty waves--- relentless in their majesty. And yet there we sit, a metropolis of individual brilliance comprised of millions of individual lights. Alone, the lights are somewhat basic, but in the context of a skyline, the impact is breath-taking. Turn off even one of the lights and the vision changes, even if it is oh-so-slightly. Turn on enough light and that light can be seen in the distant corners of space.

Tonight, our dear darling Schuyler fights to feel her light. She is a mighty warrior but almost three weeks in the ICU can be exhausting for even the mightiest of spirits. With her mouth wired shut and her eyes taped closed, you can imagine the abyss of fear and solitude. Tired of the technology, tired of the mandatory hand squeezes and thumbs up, tired of the worry, tired of the fatigue, tired of the fight--our dear Schuy cries a few more silent tears these days and seems to yearn for some form of respite or relief.

And yet, her spirit forges on. The hand squeezes are communicative and powerful. In spite of her sorrow, she champions on. And yes! Tomorrow is another BIG DAY. Tomorrow is the day that they repair her legs. We have been warned that it will be long and that it's complicated. We have also been told that once the pain from this operation is under control, Schuyler will be in warp speed.

Physical therapy for her brain, her limbs...anything that may be lagging. Within a week, we are told that they will be making her stand, walk and move. She will be pressed to breathe on her own again... to eat (albeit milkshakes but at least no more of the "chai latte" through the nostril)...within a month, who knows? But who NEEDS to know... let it suffice to say "away we go!"

So dear wonderful global family, let's each celebrate our own unique energy that creates this dazzling and powerful "city of lights"! There will be moments when we feel like the waves of the ocean are too powerful to bear-- but our individual light is not alone. We are surrounded by a community of brightness...ever powerful... brilliant...captivating... we are not alone... we are not engulfed in darkness...nor is our own light anything but integral to the completeness of the cityscape...

True, we never "know" for sure. We believe....or try to believe... we pray... we sometimes even cry... but we shine, dear Universe, we do shine! And out of tragedy sometimes emerges a beauty so profound that the lights of its brilliance takes our breath away...

Tonight as I know that I should sleep, I ask that you not only send your love to

Schuyler but send your love deep within yourself. Within each of us lives a "Schuyler" --- buoyant and beautiful-- full of hope and promise. Allow that inner child within yourself to dance, to sing, to do something totally unique to all that you are.

We are human--- which means that we are rich beyond words. We have been given the freedom to be one light or to dazzle as part of an entire city scape. I urge you to light up the sky (Schuy) today as you have never done before. Explode in your brilliance and dare any shooting star to shine any brighter...

More updates tomorrow and much love!!

Meridith

March 12, 2016

Hello, dear beautiful global family! On this Saturday morning. I feel an exhilaration that is hard to express! It is no accident that this apartment places me perfectly poised between the Heavens (37th floor), Nature (the ocean) and Humanity (the Miami skyline). I feel alert, alive and blessed beyond measure!

Three weeks ago, I was traveling toward the hospital in Socorro. Today, my darling Schuyler has officially finished her last set of procedures so the second leg of our journey begins! I'm told that the doctors are going to tackle the next phase aggressively. Within days, they hope to wean her off of the breathing tube completely so that she will be breathing on her own. From there, they will be able to work on getting her up and reacquainted with movement again. Can she see? Can she speak? Such a mountain to climb, but what is climbing a mountain when you have wings?

There will be tests and evaluations galore but there is HOPE beyond measure. The power of faith, prayers and miracles can do more than move mountains— it can create new life! And for us, each moment has become intensely and profoundly special. Each squeeze of the hand…each flutter of an eyelid cries out "LIFE!" And we are reveling in this life force!

Schuyler continues to face considerable pain due to all of these procedures, but her light shines on. The love shines on. Our strength creates a swirling vortex of strength around her and the resounding prayers, love and support of her global family coupled with the miraculous grace of this God Universe sows the seeds for a galaxy of future miracles.

As Schuyler embarks upon this new "phase" of her healing, I feel like today is a day for all of us to revel in this phenomenal process called Life. To call it a journey implies that we should be working on "getting some where", but why not simply "get" from "nowhere" to "now HERE"? The air is HERE. The waves are HERE (never to be exactly duplicated in this choreography again). The wind is HERE. The sunrise is HERE. The moment is HERE. Our love, our families, our dreams, our inspirations, our thoughts are HERE, specifically and most deliciously HERE — all lined up to keep us tapped into this one unique and precious moment.

Schuyler has the special gift of living in the moment. Savoring, basking and empowering each second— and therefore empowering each individual who passes through that second. I can't help but wonder if perhaps one of the reasons why my dear Schuy has touched so many people is precisely because we do all see the "Schuyler" within ourselves. I muse again that Schuyler's middle name is "Sachi" which means "happiness" in Japanese. How ironic to think that if I say that again using her middle name instead of the name Schuyler that it would read like this: I can't help but wonder if perhaps one of the reasons why my dear Sachi has touched so many people is precisely because we do all see the "happiness" within ourselves. To take it one step further, we all know that happiness is an integral force in Life and no force of nature or Man can crush the miracle of its momentum.

Today, as I head with such joy to the hospital to celebrate each new moment of Schuyler's life, I urge you to join us in creating your own stream of "now here" joyous moments! As the miracle of Schuyler's story proves beyond measure, we each have an inner power that can monumentally change the course of the Universe. The strength of our core can buck "reality" and create new truths. Together, we can impact love, life and humanity. We can be the change. We can be the joy.

As you continue to pray for Schuyler, revel in the gift that is your own life. Share your joys. Unleash your passion.

Rock this lovely planet! Schuy is the Limit!

Much love and thanks beyond measure,

Meridith

March 15, 2016

Hello, dear wonderful global family! It has been a whirlwind few days and I'm dashing out the door to head back to the hospital for the evening visiting hours. I will have a full update tonight but here's a sneak peek at one of the things that I will be reporting: Schuyler is now considered stable enough to be transferred OUT OF THE ICU!! How's that for an occasion for a happy dance????

Full report this evening!!! Much love, Meridith

March 16, 2016

Hello, dear glorious global family! I'm just getting back to the apartment from the hospital. Yes, perhaps the last night that dear sweet Schuyler will sleep in the ICU! So exciting!! She is officially considered "stable"! The nurses have become like family for Schuy and me so there were many, many hugs and smiles as I took my leave tonight.

Now, the perfection of the late night solitude creates a sort of magic as I contemplate sleep. Out the window to my left, the ocean is completely dark except for a few stray lights of random ships on unknown journeys. To my right, the brilliance of the lights of Miami create a poetic tapestry for my heart that just won't start racing and celebrating each heartbeat today!

Yes, Schuyler is ALIVE —brilliantly, majestically and savoring-each-breath ALIVE! Her body (and probably her mind) is exhausted from the trauma of the last three weeks but still she warriors on!

Yesterday was the first day that they tried sitting her up in the ICU's version of a "chair"—i.e. a sort of stretcher that can convert to a chair position. Back brace on, dear sweet Schuyler fought through the discomfort and sat in the chair for an hour and 15 minutes— a huge accomplishment considering that every muscle in the body sort of goes on "vacation" when you have been lying in bed for weeks on end.

Her physical therapy session today was amazing! She fought hard to work with commands to smile (can you imagine Schuyler having to work hard to smile??), move her legs, squeeze hands, move arms, wiggle her toes…a whirlwind! And she is BREATHING! She now has what is called a T-piece. This apparatus is still a tube into her throat, but it allows her to breathe 100% on her own while augmenting the natural flow of oxygen. She has been breathing on her own for more than 85 hours! How much joy a simply inhale and exhale can bring!

Dear wonderful family, Schuyler's entire healing process is not a focus on tragedy but a celebration of Life! And not just Schuyler's life, but all of our lives. Schuyler is being given the opportunity to experience a rebirth. She will not only have to relearn how to walk, how to talk and how to "live" again, but she will have the chance to reinvent herself as she ventures forward. And so do we, dear family— so do we! The rock that fell on Schuyler wasn't just a rock that impacted my sweet daughter. It was a rock that has impacted us all. Look at the power of these global prayers. Look at the insights and inspirations that so many of you are sharing. This is our chance to heal our own wounds — the ones that are less obvious than dear Schuyler's and to turn this rock into a blessing, as Schuyler would wish that it would be.

The best "gift" and "support" that we can give to Schuyler as she embarks upon this healing is to make sure that this "accident" is not for naught. Make it big.

Make it important. Open your heart and your soul and begin your own healing. Reinvent yourself. Learn to BREATHE. Learn to SEE. Learn to really LIVE LIFE. Learn to hug everyone — including yourself. Learn to MATTER — because you are uniquely important to the intricacy of this dance. Learn to have faith. Learn to believe. Learn to recognize that the rose colored lens is the ultimate "contact lens". Dare to REALLY make contact with your life…your soul! Is reality where you have been or where you will be going? Your choice, but no one drives very far using the rear view mirror.

Those of you who know me well know that I believe that the God Universe has a sense of irony and humor even in the midst of great "stress" and "tragedy". The fact that all of these major changes were initiated by a rock — i.e. that it took a boulder to "rock our world" and to show just how much of a "rock star" dear sweet Schuyler is under these circumstances— well, let's just say that I don't think that the analogy is a coincidence. This is an opportunity. I have no doubt but that Schuyler will defy all somber odds and move forward with the resolve of a champion. She WILL thrive and prosper, thanks to God, thanks to the Universe, thanks to all of your prayers and focused energy, thanks to love and thanks to her own "can't stop me now" spirit.

We "owe" it to all that we love about Schuyler to dare to face this "rock" in our own lives. Dig deep within yourself and embrace all that you are and all that you want to be. Let today be the first day in a new journey for YOU. Like Schuyler, the first steps will be baby steps and potentially accompanied by pain but power on, dear warrior family! Power on! We are magnificent creations with the magic of God and Universe behind us. Individually, we are breath-taking but when we come together like we have come together for Schuyler, we are a force that can create miracles!

Today is YOUR day! Schuy is the limit!! Much love!!

Meridith

CHAPTER 6

Force to Be Reckoned With

March 17, 2016

Newsflash! Schuyler feels your love and joy and prayers! Today, she was finally up for hearing some of your posts and videos from these FB pages! She smiles and gives them thumbs up! If you want me to share a message or a video with Schuyler tomorrow, please post it on this page! Much love! Must dash!!!!

March 20, 2016

Good morning, dear beautiful global family! What a glorious sunrise it was! Now life seems magically "abuzz" with energy! The waves tirelessly caress the shoulders of the sandy beach below my balcony. Cars zoom along the streets carrying thousands of us on some new, potentially magical journey. A slight fog cloaks the top of the downtown buildings and in one of those buildings looking like a tiny, fragile China doll lies my gorgeous Schuyler.

Schuyler's days are focused on harvesting maximum energy for each moment. Movements of her hands, toes, eyes and body that used to come without thinking must now be patiently re-learned. The challenge is beyond monumental. A month in bed has whisked away from these muscles any semblance of the power that we typically so take for granted. Schuyler must work, work, work even to recreate her "impossible to forget" smile. And yet work she does… and more work…. and more work…

We use her physical therapy times to "play". Arm reps become fantasies of consuming our favorite sushi rolls or sipping Peruvian beer. One of our dear family angels even gave her a rainbow "gripping ball". Yes, this work is hard but we still find moments for silliness, joy and laughter. Each day becomes one step closer to the dream of running up mountains like the days of old— and we feel it!

It is sometimes tempting to think that because something is hard— extremely hard— that it is impossible. However, aren't some of the most breathtaking experiences and modern conveniences born from difficulty and "impossibility"? Even electricity, for example, was born from the desperate need for more light. It was created solely because someone KNEW that this "impossible thing" was absolutely possible!

Whether it's a climb up the most majestic mountain or years spent pursuing an elusive dream, the adventure and the reward draw their richness from the presence of "struggle". Life can be "hard" but that doesn't make it "bad and it's definitely NOT impossible. A little bit of sweat can be exhilarating! It's all in your perception of the glory of the dance so leap and whirl even when it takes your breath away!

There will be falls and there may even be pain, but savor the chance to keep dancing! Embrace the chance to fully and completely LIVE— even while there is pain, because even pain is temporary. And pain can also work to make us even just a little bit stronger.

Our life has been revolving around miracles for the past month— but our lives have also been revolving around CREATING miracles. "Miracles" are only called miracles because we don't believe that certain things are possible. But what if we DO believe? A belief in God, in the Universe or even simply in the power that lies within…?

Today, Schuyler will be working to create more miracles. I would invite you on this glorious Sunday to do the same. Nurture yourself. Believe. Create. Embrace! Life is a magical opportunity to energize this glorious planet with your light! We have every ability and opportunity to leave this whirling globe just a little bit (or a LOT) better than we found it. One tiny voice in symphony with a chorus of other tiny voices can create magnificence. So sing and dance with all of your heart!! The Schuy is the Limit!

Love,

Meridith
(Schuy's mom)

March 22, 2016

Hello dear wonderful global family! So many exciting things to report with our lovely Schuyler! As you would expect, she may be still in bed but she is a force to be reckoned with! She is working on moving her hands, her fingers, her legs, toes and even eyelids. And yes, dear family, yesterday the jaw wires were removed!!!!! I confess that it was a "full of joy tears" moment because Schuyler's smile (complete with one dimple) IS BACK!!!!! Yes, you can imagine that the walls of the hospital were ROCKING with our own unique versions of the happy dance!!!

Schuyler is working on answering questions (one finger for yes and two for no) and practicing her rehab movements. The rehab is almost like Schuy's substitute for dancing— and dance she does! Her rehab team had Schuyler reclined in a therapy "chair" for two hours with great success! We do need your prayers and energy today as the team tweaks a last bit of "fine tuning" associated with her head injury. It's a steam roller of progress in our tiny hospital room and each day we get a bit closer.

Do we ever feel fear or stress or frustration or just fatigue? Of course we do! We are human beings with a wondrous treasure chest of emotions— and all of these emotions "good" and "bad" are lights on the runway leading us toward our next adventure. I truly believe that God Universe could have created one solitary person that lived a "perfect" life doing "perfect" things and thinking "perfect" thoughts if that would have served us or if it would have served our planet. So why are there so many of us here in so many "imperfect" moments? The only acceptable answer to my heart is that it is precisely our "imperfections" that lead us as individuals and us as a species to become more. It is only our desire to live better, love more and to feel better that inspires us to create and/or to evolve. And in each "flaw" lies the seeds of miraculous invention.

So what about fear? What about anger? Fear is what I call a catalyst emotion in that it cries out for action. Run… hide… or…. decide to take your power back! That might be what some would call courage— the decision to take one's power back even when your heart is pounding. And anger? Anger can be a powerful stepping stone. When one is depressed or "heart-broken" or "helpless", one has often temporarily given up one's power and assumed more of a victim's stance. Allowing oneself to feel anger can be an important bridge in taking one's power back— before then moving along to more positive emotions.

Like the colors of nature that Schuyler loves so much, our lives are a tapestry of rich and glorious emotions creating a gallery of experiences. We have a lot more control of the color of the paint and the stroke of the brush than we may think. Today, assume the stance of the artist. Choose the colors of emotion that best serve you — even if for a moment, it may need to be anger. Live. Love. Smile. Life is indeed a gift that can be savored and enjoyed in each millisecond if you allow it! As the saying goes, enjoy life's "presence" (pun of course intended). For you, my dears, are the masterpieces in motion. And this lovely planet is more spectacular than the Louvre! Today is YOUR DAY to create something wonderful! Yes, the SCHUY IS THE LIMIT!

Much love,

Meridith

March 24, 2016

Good morning dear glorious global family! What a spectacular day to be alive! A light drizzle of rain adds a sparkle to the Miami skyline and the waves of the ocean seem to tickle the shores of the ocean with additional froth this morning! Truly the perfect setting for yet another miracle to unfold!

There may be clouds overhead but there is no darkness in our hearts because yesterday afternoon, our gorgeous Schuyler actually managed to (yes) voice a very tiny yet perfect word: "hiiiiiiiii"! Her first "official greeting" in this brilliant regeneration of life!

You can IMAGINE the joy that flooded through my heart from this one simple hello from that tiny magical being that I am lucky to call my "own"!! Tears! Hugs! Squeals!! Kisses!

More tears! More hugs! And enough jumping around the room to rock the walls of every building in the Universe!

No gift could have been sweeter— or harder for Schuy to create in that moment! Still with the tubes in her throat, the only way to make sounds is through a special speech valve that redirects the air into her throat. To execute even one word requires the determination and strength of a champion. Fortunately, lovely Schuyler has become adept at filling the courageous shoes of the warrior. It required monumental effort but she spoke that lovely word 3 times! As our dear angel Amalita would say, it truly was a "Schuy High" moment (once again, the pun is very much intended—wink!).

As you read this, my dear lovely global family, I invite you to look into the mirror and recognize that a warrior champion lies within each and every one of us. Brave. Strong, Important. And always ready to truly live! Many of the great legends among humanity became superstars because someone acted as their champion. This champion often saw in them a greatness before they even saw this greatness themselves. Eventually, they themselves grew to believe in their own greatness and something "miraculous" and powerful came into being. I urge you today to be that champion! Whether you are championing others or brave enough to champion yourself, BE the one that believes today!

Be the one that sees the seeds of greatness and possesses the knowing that this seed is the start of a forest of greatness! You, dear global family, are all champions with the ability to create a galaxy of miracles. Make this the day that you step into the world as the joyous peaceful warrior, eternally ready to make your loving impact on this lovely planet that we call "home". The Schuy is the Limit!

Much love!

Meridith

CHAPTER 7

The View From the Edge

April 5, 2016

Hello dear magnificent global family! It's the end of another day and I sit here pinching myself at the beauty of it all. Aghast at life…aghast at the lights of this glorious city.. but most of all aghast at the "realness" of this specific moment in our family's unfolding. Life is a treasure…something to savor…to rejoice in.. and yes dear ones-- on occasion to be fought for…

Life is not a given. Love is not a given. But in its elusiveness it becomes a treasure. Maybe more powerful than if it was given to us in an easily accessible form of perfection.

So I promised to bring you all up to speed with all that happened last week, but forgive me if I feel the need to jump ahead. Quick synopsis: many many reasons to be joyous! Schuy still needs to sleep about 80% of the time, but when she is awake, she is TOTALLY SCHUY. Great battles are not fought easily and there are reasons that the most beautiful diamonds require a great deal of heat. So "once upon a time" this fairy princess...this sleeping beauty knew that there was a great fight to be fought... and the fight would not be gentle nor would it be quick..this was a fight that would shake her heart and test her soul...in spite of her mighty power, this would not be a battle that she could fight alone...far more magical than a fairy tale myth, this was not a fight that could be awakened by a suitor's kiss...

So here today another "first" was accomplished! With the help of three very supportive physical therapists, our darling "baby" Schuyler in her tiny little body "sat" on the edge of the bed..what an angelic vision: my daughter--every bit of her soul, her will, her body trying simply and completely to just sit upright!

There was a day for all of us when our first "sit" was cause for great celebration and I promise you that

Schuyler got to relive that moment in full "dolby sound"! Massive cheering! Arms overhead in the Yale victory pose! Smiling! Tears! Whatever might have been taking place on our gentle planet was surely stopped in its tracks for one brief moment when Schuyler "sat" on the edge of that bed!

There are most certainly things that we convince ourselves that we cannot do— often using the interpretation of someone else's words as support for this claim. In many cases, these things that we "cannot" do or be or have would be easier to achieve than the ability to sit from Schuyler's perspective right now— and yet she must persevere!

From your comments, you may laugh at what I'm about to reveal right now. Believe it or not, until I was in my late 40's I had convinced myself that I could not write. Writing was a passion that I developed in prep school. I evolved from being a pretty terrible writer into what I considered a pretty decent writer. In fact, the ultimate moment in prep school came when one of the toughest teachers in the English department walked into our class senior year and began to share the following. Women had only been admitted to Exeter for the previous 5 years when I attended school there. This teacher shared that he had his reservations about the new policy. That said, in his decades of teaching at Exeter, he had only given out 4 "A's". He shared that he had just given out his fifth "A" and ceremoniously walked over and put my paper down in front of me with that big, beautiful "A" glowing from the top of the page. I blushed beyond measure but my elation was HUGE!!

From Exeter, I went to Georgetown and even though I was interested in foreign service at the time, my love of writing inspired me to sign up for Honors English. I should share that I was not unlike the lead character in Legally Blonde at the time so I didn't always endear myself to people. In the case of my English professor at Georgetown, I think that it's safe to say that my style just wasn't her cup of tea. She asked us each to submit a sample of our writing so that she could familiarize herself with our style. OF COURSE, I submitted the paper on Solzhenitsyn's Cancer Ward that had earned me the coveted "A"! Days passed and you can imagine the pit in my stomach when she returned the paper with the grade "C+" over "D-". The same exact paper but a dramatically different assessment! I was absolutely crushed. And yes, my 17 year old brain convinced myself that I lacked all ability to write. I made it through that class and never took another English class again. Cross one major dream off of the list!

It might be possible for someone to convince dear sweet Schuyler that she couldn't walk or sit or ever dance again— but we all know that she WILL! I certainly don't blame my Georgetown English teacher for being so "hard" on me. It was my own self that told me to abandon that dream. So, today in honor of Schuyler's quest, I would urge each of us to go back and look at any of those core dreams that were tossed aside along the way.

When my Exeter guidance counselor asked me what I wanted to do when I got out of school, my answer was "to help people". I remember him looking at me with a puzzled look and then asking me if I could be a bit more specific. Ha ha! What IS your dream? What are you doing this very moment to nurture that dream? Do you treat that dream like a fairy tale or do you KNOW to the very bottom of your core that this dream WILL come to fruition?

Today, live your dream! BE that dreamer! See that dream in the face of every loved one and every stranger! Yes of course— at moments, the plausibility of that dream may seem like Schuyler's first attempt to "sit" on the edge of that hospital bed— but sitting is the first step toward leaping!

You are most DEFINITELY put here on this lovely planet with a soul FULL of dreams for a reason! To share one of Schuy and my favorite quotes (by Ellen Johnson Sirleaf): If your dreams don't scare you, they are not big enough! So dream those dreams and live "dangerously"!

Today is the perfect day to relaunch an old dream or to start something new! Dive in! Today is your ocean! Splash in those waves and get ready to grab your surf board! The Schuy is the Limit!!!

Much Love,

Meridith

CHAPTER 8

"Real-Eyes" the Rehab

April 10, 2016

Hello dear glorious global family! UNBELIEVABLE NEWS!! So much to say that I couldn't finish it all yesterday morning! Solution? You will get two days worth of updates— and the updates are jaw- dropping!!

[Written this morning} Greetings from an absolutely PERFECT morning in Miami! The breeze is delicately wafting through the open sliding door here on the 37th floor of our little haven. The chilly air feels like a cooling massage on every inch of my skin as I sit here. The turquoise tone of the ocean soothes and calms and the obvious joy of two lone wakeboarders who are navigating the waves feels like the perfect way to start the perfect morning!

Yes, dear family, I have MAJOR MAJOR breaking news: SCHUYLER was officially transferred to the rehab center on Friday evening!! The t-piece with its highway of annoying (but oh so precious) tubes was removed and Schuyler was passed ceremoniously on to the next phase of care! Even one of our favorite members of the neuro team looked slightly teary eyed. What an amazing moment!

The excitement began early when Schuyler's speech therapist arrived to see if Schuyler can begin to learn to swallow again. Three tiny teaspoons of orange juice and one tiny teaspoon of apple sauce later, it was as if Schuyler had hiked up a mountain— these first monumental little, little swallows were four gigantic teaspoons of success! The feeding tube with her "chai latte" diet will definitely stay in for a while longer, but the day will surely come when we all sit together at a gigantic sushi table— I am positive!!!

The day continued with the usual ration of conversation interspersed with TONS of rest. There were some fun, giggly moments opening some special gifts from friends— a fabulous "Schuy is the Limit" poster from Camp Scoutcrest and a goodie box filled with everything from audio books to scarves from a dear friend of mine. Lots of smiles and lots of rest!

Suddenly, in late afternoon, Schuy's lead doctor arrived to share the results of the early morning CAT scan. Yes, the patch of air that had been worrying them inside her cranium had miraculously disappeared. How many times have I heard the word "miraculous" during this journey??!! That one amazing word has surely become my best friend in this new life-bearing vocabulary!

With the outlook of an additional procedure now improbable, Schuy was clear to FINALLY get rid of the t-piece! HUGE Schuyler smile!! While there is no question but that this ventilating system had played a critical role in her healing, the network of tubes and suction obviously had grown to feel like torture to dear sweet Schuyler. Thank goodness she would finally be free!!!

There was one thing that the doctor wanted me to see so I followed them out of Schuy's room into the nurse's station. There was a pronounced lesion on the top central part of Schuy's brain. Initially, because Schuyler was responding so well to commands, the neurology team had thought that it must be an aberration in the scan. As the swelling went down it became apparent to the team that, as unbelievable as it might seem, this lesion was very, very real. I wasn't sure why they wanted me to see this at this point. The lead doctor looked deeply into my eyes and must have sensed my confusion. He said that what is so incredulous about that lesion is that almost never do patients with that type of lesion even wake up— much less interact and progress like Schuyler has. He emphasized that this particular floor has many, many patients who have this type of lesion and who will probably never "come back". To see Schuyler vibrant and healing is yet again to view another miracle.

I confess that this information struck a chord in my heart—another sweet embrace from the God Universe that humbled me beyond measure. I couldn't get back to my darling Schuy's room fast enough! Sweet darling little Schuyler was lying there in her bed with her one eye open and fidgeting with her legs so full of hope and determination. Coldplay's Yellow was playing on Pandora (OF COURSE-- since by now I am used to the world serenading me with its magically synchronized playlist) and the magnitude of all these miracles shined brilliantly down upon me. Little Schuyler. Little me. So many, many prayers answered! So many, many miracles to embrace in just a matter of months!

I blurted out a bit of what the doctor said and held her little chin in my hand. "Thank you, Schuyler! Thank you for coming back to me!! Neither you or I are done with life yet and we are strongest together! We can't go anywhere when we have this tiny wonderful world to 'change', right?!!" She smiled and wiggled her hand toward mine. I of course immediately linked my fingers in hers and with the grip of a thousand kisses, she squeezed my hand.

As hard as it was to execute, little Schuy began leaning that delicious shaved head toward me and we shared a few well deserved tears of love and awe. Both she and I were very much "here" in that moment! We were living, loving and vibrant--and in the magnitude of that moment we KNEW that our lives will never be the same— nor should it be!

Within 30 minutes, one of the doctors on the team and our favorite PA arrived to do the procedure of removing the T-piece. (HUGE YIPPEEE OF DELIGHT AND AMAZEMENT FROM MY HEART!!!) I stepped outside of the door and heard lots of coughing and then all of a sudden the doctors were calling for me! I raced back inside the room and they had capped the traech with a speech valve and Schuyler was straining to talk!!! A very loud "HI" resonated from her gorgeous lips! The room erupted with victory signs, spontaneous happy dances and huge smiles! Not to mention, on Schuyler's part a HUGE sigh of relief and exhaustion! She almost immediately dozed into the most blissful of sleeps— finally, for the first time in months, unencumbered by a network of tubes and invasive valves!

I thought that we were done for the evening but as I peered out of the room, my two neuro heroes were walking back to me with more huge smiles saying, "guess what… best news ever: the rehab team has accepted Schuyler! She is going to be moving to rehab within the hour!!" Not to sound like the Kardashians, but OMG!!! Omg!! Omg!! More hugs!

More happy dances and feeling like a puppy with the best toy ever!!!

I ran BACK to the room and began the now familiar process of packing up the happiness! Posters, pictures and banners came off the wall and into bags, baskets and hampers! OMG! How is this possible! Two weeks earlier than expected Schuyler is off to rehab???!!

[Tonight] Ah, dear glorious family, it is past midnight and I am back on the terrace on the 37th floor soaking in the wonder of life and the energy of our sparkling planet! Life, hopes and dreams surround me with every spec of light on the horizon. The waves, the sounds, the lights continue to pulse with the continuity of a heartbeat. Our world is alive and beating with purpose, hope and energy. I hear the sounds of voices on a balcony below me— a different language but so alive, so immersed in their own unique journey.

And Schuyler! Oh my goodness! when I arrived at the rehab center, Schuyler was finally in something resembling real clothes… a tee-shirt from the South Beach life guards and some paper trousers from the rehab center. She looked fragile but as regal as any global princess! Of course all of Schuyler's clothes are scattered around the world at this point— Peru, Tampa…anywhere but Miami! Ha ha! Yes, for a while, her wardrobe will be improvised but it will be the happiest collection of garments that she has ever worn!

She was in a variation of a wheelchair—exhausted by the early morning "occupational therapy" (i.e. the closest thing to a bath that she has enjoyed in more than a month), She was immediately off to one then two physical therapies! Wow, what a day for our warrior princess! I arrived with one of her closest friends and of course in spite of her fatigue, she gave him a huge smile.

She still can bear no weight on her left leg and no weight on her arms due to the scapula injuries but she was determined to fight and master these therapy sessions. By the time that we were finished, she had viewed herself in a full length mirror for the first time and managed to sit upright TOTALLY on her own 6 times for about 15-45 seconds each time! The things that most of us take for granted are like climbing Mt. Everest for sweet Schuy right now.

And yet, Schuyler continues to smile and persist. Schuy's new therapist today said Schuy has already earned a reputation among the therapists. She affectionately said that Schuy is being referred to as "mighty mouse"! Tiny but able to rock the world! So be it but amen!

As I sit here tonight, I reach out to each of you with the thought that we are never so small that we cannot absolutely ROCK THIS WORLD. One itsy bitsy tiny voice—one little "hhhhiiiiii"-- can shake an entire Universe. And yes, dear global family, perhaps with the right magic, miracles ARE easy. Whether it's your strong connection with God or simply your connection with faith, love and belief—when tuned in and tapped into that "magic" we humans can "conquer" logic. We can go way beyond the statistics of "reality".

So as the lights pulse and shine around this amazing city, I muse… and because you are now my family you know that I play with words…so into my musing comes the word "realize"…what if we moved the cards around a bit and said instead "Real Eyes-ed". What if realized meant that we finally and completely opened our souls to truly"see" even that which we believe to be "impossible". Do we have to see if first for it to be real or do we believe it first and then it becomes real? Can we finally see the potential in every moment with our REAL EYES?!

Dear sweet wonderful family, life is such a gift! And there are so many miracles (with smaller versions that we call coincidences)! We beg to understand them! We cry out at times to know their meaning! But dear sweet loved ones, what if the monumental moments are not the destinations and things to "write home about"? What if it's our "chronic thoughts" that define how AND WHAT we live? Isn't that string of "random moments" actually the life that we are living?

Oh dear! So many of us may panic at this thought and think that (there it is again) that we are "failing"to control our own "destiny"… but dear sweet ones, YES, let's return to savoring the moment and to the knowing that there is a sublime and divine "rightness" to the history that we each have lived.

Let's "real eyes"our dreams…let's "real eyes" our belief in the beauty of each moment and in our tiny planet. If miracles upon miracles can bless our sweet Schuyler's soul and body, why not bless our planet?

It's late and as I conclude this post, I shiver with excitement. Dear darling family, do you realize how many of us that there are? Look at your dreams with "real eyes" and all that you/we CAN indeed believe into reality. We have only the power that we believe that we have, so it's time to BELIEVE AND BELIEVE IMMENSELY. Miracles are only called miracles because the general consensus is that that they rarely come true. Respectfully, I beg to differ.

We—yes WE— have the opportunity to initiate change in this beautiful world. I would ask of you today to look into the mirror and simply (1) say that you LOVE you and then (2) to say that you individually are powerful and that your own UNIQUELY BEAUTIFUL shine CAN change the world. Then walk outside and spread your love onto the first random stranger that you see… Say it! Find the Schuy within yourself that helps the random stranger love themselves….because this beautiful Schuyler essence lives within everyone.

Dear global family…. within each of you lives a miracle waiting to be unleashed… the schuy is the limit… we SO want to hear you roar~~

Much love and happy, HAPPY Sunday!

Meridith

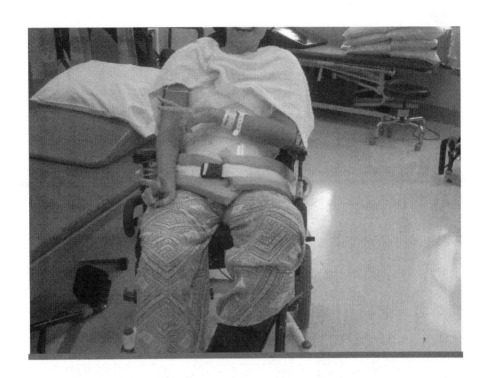

CHAPTER 9

37th Heaven

Saturday, 4/16/16

Hello dear glorious global family! I confess that when I wrote this, I was probably awake a bit later than I should have been so once again, here is a bit of a "hybrid update" from Thursday night and this afternoon. Let me apologize right now for its length because if you had told me last Friday where Schuy would be today, even I would have wondered how that would be possible! But I'm jumping ahead.... wink! So here we go, dear family....maybe one of the most amazing updates yet....!

Thursday: Greetings from my 37th floor haven where the roar of the waves outside the open sliding door melds with the whoosh of the cars zooming by on their great rush to reach an important "somewhere". The majestic thunder of a plane overhead crescendos and then quickly dwindles into a peaceful drone as hundreds of other souls make their way to their own proclaimed "destinations". We are all going somewhere, aren't we... and though we do grow older, it seems like we never quite outgrow the childhood urge to demand, "are we there yet?"

Schuyler's rehab officially started on Monday. On Saturday, she was "evaluated". She was put in a wheel chair and transported to three different team members who charted a base line of her strength, flexibility, ability to speak and to swallow. They got her out of the chair briefly to determine whether she could hold her head up on her own and whether she can lift either of her arms on her own. Remember that the "big achievement" last week was sitting in the hospital gurney "chair" for three hours at about a 30 degree incline. Sitting upright and being asked to support her head and her own weight in a sitting posture— well, that seemed to be asking MOUNTAINS of her! Yet that's exactly what they did.

Sunday was a day of rest. Schuyler would occasionally say the word "hi" or the phrase "I love you" but even without all of the tubes, talking was an obvious chore. Communication was still almost entirely via answers to yes or no questions using shakes of the head or hand signals. She was super exhausted and slept most of the day. We were excited to see how much she moved in her bed though. Her left arm could inch its way to her head to fend off an itch. Yay! And the crazy flexibility of her legs plus the constant pointing of the toes on her "free" foot — obviously, her many years of training at New Tampa Dance Theatre was still paying off! Little steps that we pinned our hearts on. Progress! Small steady beacons of hope that lit up her room like fireworks!

On Monday, the rocket ship called rehab thoroughly launched! The format is pretty simple yet formidably grueling: forty-five minutes of occupational therapy, forty-five minutes of physical therapy, forty-five minutes of speech therapy (which includes the use of the mouth for consuming food) followed by an hour and a half of recuperation time. There is a half hour break for "lunch" (which in Schuy's case was still the feeding tube) then the "work beyond the

point where you drop" (camouflaged ingeniously as fun) continues for one more session of occupational therapy and a final session of physical therapy.
 Finally, in mid-afternoon, these rehab warriors are returned to their rooms where they typically collapse into a cocoon of exhaustion. Yes, I have literally seen rehab patients fall asleep in the middle of their exercises, but apparently this level of intensity is one key to this program's success. And success they do have!

On Monday around noon, the final remnants of Schuyler's tracheostomy were removed. Yet another step closer to total freedom from the world of tubes! It was hard not to shed a tear of joy looking down on that tiny little face "one step closer" to feeling "whole"! All that remained of the tracheostomy was a bit of gauze and bandage. How far away the days of the ventilators now seemed…

I think that the release of the tracheostomy was a powerful emotional metaphor for both of us. It signified the true "departure" of the ICU "era" and the first step into the world of who she would now "be" and how she would become that. I stayed well into that evening on Monday. Schuy seemed restless in her bed. She was moving her legs against the side of the bed constantly and sighing deep sighs. I asked if she felt pain. She nodded yes. I asked where she felt pain: her head? No. Her legs? No. Her stomach? No. Her eyes were closed. I stopped a moment and just tried to "connect" with her. A very long pause. "Schuyler, is your pain anxiety? Are you worried?" She nodded her head yes— and a floodgate of healing tears began to flow from both of us.

Over the rails of the hospital bed, I buried my head against her tiny chest and felt her little arm fight its way up behind me and over so that she could give my head a huge hug. Our first true, genuine, blissful, physical hug since the rock struck in February!

"Schuyler, it's ok! I think that we have earned a huge cry at this point so why don't we just stop trying to be strong for a moment and just be together a big gigantic cry!?" I felt both of our bodies release the resistance and cry we did! Tears of life! Tears of gratitude! Tears of togetherness! She had survived and what we are now to live will never be the same. Our rocket had broken out through the outer layers of the atmosphere and what we were now gazing upon was an entire galaxy versus our prior perspective from the tiny orbiting object below. We had no choice. We had made it this far. Now we must suit up and go!

By Tuesday morning, she was being pushed to speak rather than to use gestures to communicate. She was able to swallow small bits of water, apple sauce and saltines soaked in apple sauce. A mere three days earlier, she could barely manage a couple drops of water! A "swallow test" was ordered for Wednesday. This would give them a more clear concept of whether they could finally consider removing the feeding tube! Basically, the last remaining tube in her little body!

This 109 pound young woman who could barely hold her head up on her own on Friday was now sitting upright on the edge of a padded platform for 1 minute then 30 seconds then 30 seconds more then 30 seconds more. A game of matching letters to the letters on the board became an epic struggle to simultaneously rekindle coordination, strength and concentration. Reach, Schuyler! Reach!

Amazingly, she had little trouble with the neuro psychologists' exam. She even managed to subtract 7 from 100 "then do it again then do it again then do it again then do it again"— all the way until the psychologist finally stopped in the 60's.

By 4pm, she was beyond exhausted! Bed! Bed! If she could have had any wish at that moment, it would simply have been to collapse into that hospital bed!

When I left on Tuesday evening, she would reluctantly gather the energy to maybe utter a phrase or two. She would sigh and roll her eyes playfully when I would tell her to try to express her words. And more often than not, when she WOULD try, it was like a farcical version of charades. I would be guessing words and she would shake her head no. "You hurt your toe?" (No) "You want to go?" (No) "You have an itch on your nose?" (No!!) Typically, we would just collapse into fits of laughter and realize that we weren't quite at the point of being able to communicate just yet! At least, neither of us was taking the other too seriously! In spite of our fatigue, we were managing to make this fun! Little did I know that our laughter was the God Universe's way of welcoming us to our next MAJOR turning point!

I arrived on Wednesday morning to find Schuyler's mouth covered by a respiration therapy mask and absolutely stopped in my tracks. The boom box was blaring oldies. "Saint" Nick, one of the great guys on the physical therapy team was standing there grinning. The respiratory therapist was beside HIM laughing AND MISS SCHUYLER was chattering away, singing song lyrics and laughing the type of delicious infectious laughter that is typically reserved for infants!

Apparently, in the wee hours of the morning, she embraced the joy of having a beloved voice again! And she hadn't stopped talking since! It was a miraculous yet sweetly playful moment that brought a mixture of whoops and tears to all of us. To those of us observing her, it was HUGE. Yet to Schuyler, it was but a fully lived moment— so purely "now", so purely savored that anyone observing her had no choice but to gasp in awe!

I will continue the rest of the week's updates tomorrow (YES, THERE IS MORE!!!), but for now, I sit here soaking in the glow of appreciation for almost two entire months ABSOLUTELY FILLED WITH MIRACLES! In a world where miracles are labelled "rare"....!

And my mind dances… this thing that we call Life… measured in segments of time… centuries, decades, years, days, minutes, seconds… but equally measured quite often by the number of "achievements" and "monumental moments that one has lived…

So what about these monumental moments in our lives? Is this why we zoom around in our cars? Or travel great distances around the globe? Is this why we plan and set goals? Focus on success? Aim higher? Accumulate more? IS our life only as great as the number of monumental moments that we achieve? Are therefore 10 marriages (marriages being one form of monumental achievement) in a lifetime the sign of more happiness than just one? Hee hee! And when do we "know" that we have arrived — and oh yes… then what?

Now don't get me wrong, I too LOVE monumental achievements! As you might guess, I don't think that 10 marriages are better than one. OF COURSE the monumental moments are huge and they are to be savored to the deepest, richest extent possible— but in watching dear sweet Schuyler, it strikes me that as sweet as those monumental moments are, it's the "nondescript" moments of uncontrollable laughter that define whether we are "living a happy life" or not. It's the huge number of hugs in your day, the huge volume of moments when you feel inspired and exhilarated by all that you are doing. It's the frustration that "magically transforms" into that moment of your greatest inspiration! It's the first thought of the morning being one of joy and excitement. It's battling through the fatigue with a smile and an enthusiasm that one is even still in the game. It's loving the entire process even when we don't always quite understand it.

As I sit next to my sweet "exhausted beyond belief" Schuy, it definitely strikes me that happiness isn't something that "happens" nor is it something that you find or something that you earn. Happiness is "a given". Yes a "given"! It is as available as the oxygen in our atmosphere—invisible yet always there for the "living"--if you will but "real-eyes" it and willingly then take it on as your own". As I observe it in my days with Schuy, happiness is almost like an additional sense, perhaps a bit more discreet than sight,sound, touch or taste. When you awaken it, you carry it with you wherever you go.

And so, dear global family, as you zoom across the Universe toward your oh-so glorious destination, hold tight to that "one personal item" that is indeed the small but mighty treasure called happiness. Aim for the stars with all of your heart, but learn to find great joy in the rocket ship that will take you there! It's of course about the triumph of the success—but it's equally about how many times did you explode with laughter when you so obviously "failed"?!

So as the lights in this glorious cityscape outside my window perhaps dim a bit and as I listen to the persistent buzz of humanity still on the move at 1AM, I urge you to LIVE your days exploding with joy! Sing along with your own personal boom box! Turn a few unsuspecting heads! Laugh at your "failures". But perhaps most of all, savor not only those steps that appear to be HUGE but also those steps that may initially appear to be small or even (gasp) grotesquely BACKWARDS... because, dear family, without the occasional step backward there is no dance—and without the dance, there would be no grand ballet! Life in all of its glorious whirling momentum is why we step onto the dance floor to begin with. And once you begin to move (yes) the Schuy is the Limit!!!

Much love,

Meridith

CHAPTER 10

Take Over Control

April 22, 2016

Hello dear wondrous global family! Well the technology elves were creating mischief for me this week. My computer went on a watery cruise from which it could not return. I'm back in action now though so I will share with you the post that was to be posted on Schuy is the Limit last Sunday!

(Written on April 17) I'm sitting here in Schuyler's room in the rehab wing feeling deliciously relaxed and at peace. The sound of the nurses laughter out in the hall and of the John Mayer channel on the Pandora create the perfect backdrop for Schuyler's day of rest before the launch of week 2 of rehab. So much has happened so quickly— infinitely faster than even I would have imagined!

My last post left us at Wednesday morning—virtually half way through the first week of the rehab adventure! In just a few short days, I saw Schuyler grow from barely able to sit on the gurney "chair" to the point where she can sit up and support herself for minute after minute. She is gaining slow but steady arm strength so that she can already participate in feeding and grooming herself. Her shoulders and right arm are definitely SORE! Angel Amalita saved us with the gift of some sore muscle cream and we're applying it like body lotion these days— but still Schuyler persists with laughter and a smile!

But even Schuyler is not without her moments of (let's just say) "naughtiness". Hee hee! Yes, dear global family, in spite of the über mittens capturing her fingers, dear sweet Schuyler managed to pull out her feeding tube on the morning of her swallow test. Nothing like giving yourself a wee bit of pressure to pass it—but that's Schuyler!

As I had mentioned, Schuyler had barely begun rekindling her ability to use those swallowing muscles. On Wednesday, they would take her back over to the West Wing for a special x-ray look at her throat muscles in action. The test was scheduled for 1:30pm but it was after 3pm by the time that we headed over. Schuyler was already so exhausted that she fell asleep on the transport gurney!

When she was wheeled into the radiology room, Schuy was in deep sleep and in no mood to attempt swallowing. The speech therapist tried waking her by touching her and talking to her, but Schuyler was persistent in her desire to sleep. I tried speaking to her but then had an idea. I had my phone and my iPad with me so I asked if they would mind if I put on some music. If it would wake up dear Schuy, they were totally fine with it. I opened my iTunes and Titanium (of course) popped right up.

I started singing along and mentioned that Jasmine Thompson had sent a special video message to Schuyler. One of the techs asked how that happened and before I knew it the entire room of about 9 technicians and therapists were listening intently to the story of Schuyler's playlist in the Colombian ICU. "Wow! That gave me chills!" one of the nurses said and suddenly the vibe in the room began shifting noticeably lighter.

Schuyler was starting to wake up but she was still not totally energized so when Titanium finished, I switched immediately to Afrojack! Our "workout music"! What happened next was surreal! Not only were the nurses and technicians dancing along to "I Want You to Take Over Control" but little Schuyler began bopping her shoulders and singing! There were cheers, laughter and the room now felt alive with energy! If you took away the medical equipment, we could easily have been chilling in one of Miami's posh DJ clubs. Schuyler was ready!

The west wing team put Schuy into the chair of the x-ray machine and in just a few short minutes of swallowing everything from water to "apple sauce soaked" crackers, Schuyler had PASSED her swallow test! More jumping! More high fives!! And of course a major squeal and hug to Schuy on my part!!!

When we got back to rehab, word had already spread and the nurses were running up to the gurney and congratulating Schuyler! The doctor came in to Schuyler's room and although everyone was encouraged by the results, she very sweetly but firmly communicated that it was unlikely that Schuyler would be able to properly eat enough food to satisfy the nutritional and caloric requirements. On Thursday morning, they would still most likely have to put a feeding tube back in. Another steep mountain to climb, but they would certainly give her the chance to eat enough calories on her own.

Food at this point meant strictly liquids and purées but if I could get Schuyler to eat this meant that as of Wednesday, April 13, Schuyler was officially TUBE FREE for the first time since February 19th!!!! To see that beautiful face without the feeding tube dangling from her nose was more exhilarating than I can begin to express!! I couldn't stop kissing her!! And she couldn't stop saying, "Yay! Yay! Crazy, RIGHT???"

By 6pm, a tray featuring everything from puréed fish to soup and apple juice had been delivered to Schuyler's room.

All liquids had to be thickened and everything had to be consumed via spoon, even if it was a beverage. I confess that I was a bit nervous about feeding her so fortunately for the first meal one of our favorite nurses came to oversee and assist me. Believe it or not, our sweet Schuyler was not a huge fan of the idea of puréed fish or jello, but with a bit of coaxing, she managed to consume an entire cup of apple juice and the luke warm tomato soup. We were on our way!

On Thursday, still no new feeding tube so I got permission to embellish with my own home made concoctions as long as they were puréed. I was told that I could indulge her with Jamba Juice and milk shakes as long as I could get her to eat!

Fortunately, we have always been healthy eaters and Schuyler got a huge incredulous laugh from her therapists when she lamented how much she missed her kale! Needless to say, I immediately ran to Jamba Juice for Thursday's fare and I was up early the next morning puréeing tuna, quinoa, brown rice and of course making a couple of different flavors of smoothie.

By the weekend, we had still dodged the feeding tube "bullet" and Schuyler was happily consuming my concoctions! I even managed to indulge her with some creative purées of dessert favorites— i.e. miniature vegan cupcakes! My dad and his wife Kathy and my half sister Jenny were down to celebrate my dad's birthday so with the help of a mini blender, I managed to purée a mini red velvet cupcake and a vanilla cupcake for her! It's amazing what you can "whip up" (pun intended) when the potential of a feeding tube is looming!

[Today is Friday and almost two weeks have passed. I am thrilled to say that we are still feeding tube free here in Sunshine Girl's room! And Schuyler is glowing!]

Physically, Schuyler continues to make great strides! Last Friday, with the help of her PT team and a miracle machine, Schuyler "stood" for the first time in almost two months. She had a huge smile and said "oh my gosh! That's the first time that I have stood up in almost 5 days!!" Needless to say, we all roared and pointed out to her that it had actually been just a wee bit longer than that! Another huge smile with the reply, "That's CRAZY!" More happy tears! More pinching myself as I try to absorb how far we have come in less than two months!!

And what a delicious world it truly is! Rediscovering "old tricks" and rekindling the things that she so loves! We have discovered the most unexpected things like the fact that Schuyler remembers sign language! When I asked her about it, she nonchalantly told me that she had learned it for a project at IDS (now Corbett Academy). Yes, middle school!! She remembers passwords and intricate specifics and even her short term memory (typically a challenge for patients recovering from brain injuries) is coming along.

Our days are full of passion. We have laughed. We have cried. We have sung endless songs together— from U2's "With or Without You" to "Superfreak", courtesy of Miami's "newest beach station" to Taylor Swift. Schuyler thrives these days on music!

We can already feel the love of this rehab team— from the amazingly charismatic doctor who says "I love you all" to her staff as she leaves for the evening to the therapists, nurses and technicians. This is a magical place where anything is possible—and we of course intend to continue to create the "I'm possible"!

And always the intriguing presence of this miracle beyond all miracles! Even the doctors and nurses are now revealing their awe. Last week we had two profound revelations from the Jackson team and yet as often now as I have heard about all the odds that we have defied, I never cease to feel the immensity of this inexplicable reality. With much of the adrenaline now behind me, I find that I am now more often moved to joyous tears than when we were in the "dire throes" of the accident. What a journey this is!

In the Jackson system, there are a group of nurses that "float" from one wing to the next so there are several nurses who saw Schuy when she had just arrived in the ICU and who have had the chance to see her now. One of the nurses here in rehab actually "happened to have been" (are we still calling these developments coincidences—wink) Schuyler's nurse during her last week in the west wing. As she saw Schuyler sitting without assistance last Wednesday (versus only a week earlier when Schuy could barely tolerate reclining at 45 degrees on the gurney chair), she shared with me that Schuyler is amazing them all. In all of her decades with the hospital, she considers Schuy one of the top two miracle cases that she has ever seen. As you know, I have always KNOWN that this would be "our miracle"— and yet the magnitude of emotion came precisely from the "knowing" that I have felt all along that it could not have been any different. "Miracles are only miracles because people believe that they are not possible…"

Another face to face with the "miracle of it all" occurred on Friday. We had gotten Schuyler into her "wheel throne" (a larger more "ornate" version of a wheel chair) when in walked the amazing surgeon who had lead the maxillofacial reconstructive team. I hadn't seen him since his post op report on March 4th. Trust me, he is truly one of the best of the best. What he and his team had to overcome was formidable. And yet, this phenomenal man who has performed thousands upon thousands of surgeries stood in little Schuyler's room watching her speak saying little else but, "that's amazing! No... that's really, really amazing...!" This surgeon who has seen decades of cases was stopped in his tracks at the magnitude of Schuyler's success. Yes, dear family, there sat living, singing proof that Life does not always adhere to textbook statistics.

And so, my dear darling global family, I urge you to take a step back...breathe and soak it all in. I can't help but muse about the outcome of this all. These doctors have performed hundreds and in some cases thousands of procedures on far less difficult cases, so I am told. Remember that multiple doctors have now told me that Schuy's case was one of the most difficult cases ever. By text book logic, Schuyler should not have made it— or if she had "made it", the medical world data supported a future in a vegetative state— or maybe best case scenario, in a state of major paralysis. And oh by the way, the original prognosis was that she would not be able to see. And most certainly she would not be able to smell. Well, yes, dear family, Schuyler can see and we learned this week that she can "inexplicably" smell!

How do we explain what happened here? These are the same doctors who have worked on thousands of patients—genius talent but still typically results that reflect medical expectation. So what was different here? My dear darling family, I would have to say that the difference was in the collection of prayers and love and energy that surrounded dear sweet Schuyler combined with the KNOWING of those of us who were close to her that this was but the first step in her "second journey".

So in other words, it wasn't anything that we each physically "did" that achieved these results and it wasn't that these doctors did something special for Schuyler that they don't do for other patients. So what is the variable in this scenario? Could it be that the major difference was the positivity and global prayers that surrounded our warrior? What if the only possible explanation is that the combination of minds/prayers/energy CAN and DOES make a difference. Isn't that an idea worth pondering?

Without "doing" anything (other than directing our thoughts and prayers), we all helped to "create" this miracle that defies "reality". We shifted the course of the future. Based on "precedent", Schuyler as she now sits in that room should simply not be "possible"....

So what if....? What if we can each start to BELIEVE in this sort of "magic"? What if we can direct this level of faith, belief, energy, knowing and prayer to other "impossible" issues on our tiny planet? What if we were to direct them toward world hunger, world peace or the other gaps in love and abundance that we would love to impact? Impossible your brain may say? But Schuyler's return to health was also thought to be impossible so doesn't it follow that if one "impossible" miracle (actually in Schuyler's case numerous miracles) can exist, then infinite number of miracles could exist?

Today, I would urge you to focus on our revolving planet as you did on Schuyler— not as a tiny planet that is mortally wounded, but as a huge garden of beauty and possibility. Schuyler had multiple broken bones, but we focused on her glory. She had injuries that many thought would never heal— but they ARE healing "in spite of" the odds. This world and our fellow beings have FAR MORE wondrous aspects than it does imperfections. Today, I urge you to go out and see the beauty in this Schuyler-esque planet. Look for its greatness and expect its magnificent future. KNOW that you play a HUGE ROLE in this journey and that your power is immense. Smile, run, dance, and revel in the moment. We CAN create miracles. We ARE creating miracles. We DO make a difference in this lovely planet with each and every belief. EMBRACE your uniqueness and LOVE this glorious dance called Life. We are here for a reason and THE SCHUY IS THE LIMIT!

Much love,

Meridith

CHAPTER 11

A Thousand Years

April 28th, 2016

Hello dear sweet amazing global family!

Life could not be more powerful— more filled with profoundly vibrant moments— or moving at a faster momentum! Welcome to the terrifying magnificence of opting to really surf the waves of Life! Scary! Crazy! Fragile yet strong! "Twilight Saga —A Thousand Years" wraps around my heart via Pandora. Wow! I stand here engulfed in yet another Miami nightscape that blasts through any definition of normal that ever existed two months earlier... Intoxicating! And just when I thought that this vision could not POSSIBLY be any more thrilling, I am greeted with (yes) FIREWORKS exploding over the water on the beach! Life is truly celebrating not simply the "rebirth" of my darling Schuyler, but perhaps the rebirth of my own inner child. How do I process all of this? All of the miracles….all of the love… all of the newness? And the captivating resonance of these powerful waves…. what a planet…!

Progress with our princess warrior has been immense! Fighting to relearn to swallow, fighting to relearn to chew, fighting to relearn to sit without falling, fighting to relearn to enunciate, fighting to progress to an independent wheelchair, fighting to relearn the skills that most of us achieve without consciously trying. And yet, our dear sweet Schuy manages to turn these "battles" into a glorious, miraculous dance—- deep concentration and effort followed by that "take your breath away" single-dimple grin…! And oh the exhaustion and constant aches and fatigue! Her 5 hours of therapy leave her completely drained of energy and begging simply for bed— but the strength is returning! As her Fairy Grandmother Gammy would say, "Inch by Inch is a cinch. Yard by yard, it's hard." Schuyler seems determined to conquer twelve of those inches at a time and yet there is always a "please", "thank you", a glowing smile and an "I love you" for everyone who is assisting us along this ultimate bootcamp journey.

So much love in the midst of this process! Even the rehab doctor stopped me in the hall to say, "do you KNOW how much I love you?!" When you bring love and joy to a moment— no matter how challenging that moment may be— you'd be surprised how powerfully Life mirrors that love back to you. On Monday, Schuyler, Saya and I ventured outside again this time with two of Schuy's therapists! What a gorgeous day it was! Schuyler was stopping traffic in her wide brimmed straw hat and sunglasses, perched like a tiny China doll in her wheel chair. As we wheeled across the cobble stone toward the Au Bon Pain and a "chunky monkey" chocolate peanut butter milk shake, we saw two workers patching up the cement on the walkway. We greeted them and before we knew it, they invited us to write Schuyler's name in the cement! I of course took them up on it and by the time that Schuyler had her shake, "Schuy is the Limit" had been written in the cement for all to see! Schuy was beaming and remarking, "Awwww, that's so cool!"

On Tuesday, we went back out to that same path and discovered that our signature had been smoothed over. Ha ha! No writing in the cement today, but the Universe had different treasures for us. It was a spectacular day that we celebrated by indulging in a little Wallaby yogurt "picnic" in one of the hospital grounds' gardens. More giggles. More yogurt. FaceTime with her lovely sister and plenty of time to once more savor the kiss of the sunshine and the caress of the breeze. The grand finale of this lovely excursion came as we approached our building's entrance. Two absolutely exquisite yellow and black butterflies surrounded us in a joyous aerial ballet. Joined by a third butterfly, they literally whirled and flitted around us for more than a minute. It was as if the Universe was circling us in yet another joyous dance of Life and celebration in the heart of this urban environment. It was as if every drop of this planet was aligned to cheer us on as we both take our own unique "first steps" in this exhilarating journey. I expected this "healing process" to be an evolution for Schuyler. Who would have thought that it would become a sort of rebirth for me as well?

"Life" changes. We change. And actually that is the (albeit sometimes painful) beauty of each of us. We grow. We blossom. We wonder. We ask. We feel it—those answers— and often the answers are not what we hope to feel...we recoil... we question...and yet, we know.... brilliantly and frighteningly that we must take that step forward...oh please no...and yet magnificently yes.....!

How do I explain...how do I capture this new world that Schuyler and Saya and Ryu/Linden and I tread upon? There is no returning to "normal" because normal is like driving using the rear view mirror. And how do I convey that we actually feel blessed to be given this gift? So many moments filled with laughs, hugs, huge embraces...even the occasional tears... yes, dear global family, from the threat of near death, we are all relearning how to LIVE....passionately and perfectly so..

Life promises each and every one of us a dazzling and unique journey! Each chapter with profound and often unseen value! Dare to dream as largely and powerfully as you can—while remembering as you walk calmly and confidently toward those dreams that the moments that you truly LIVE while you pursue those dreams are as BIG as any monumental vision that your imagination can conjure. "Are we there yet?" The answer is always YES— you ARE there—regardless of where that "there" may be.

Dance with the butterflies! Pass a smile to a stranger! Embrace the YOU of this moment that is steadily and magnificently unfolding! Today is a day of perfect change, perfect opportunity. Feel the invitation from Life to hop on the board and surf those gloriously relentless waves! Even if the waves knock you off, your surf board will be waiting, always ready to take you on that next awe-inspiring adventure! We love you. The Schuy is the Limit!

Much love,

Meridith

CHAPTER 12

The Great
Tapestry

May 3, 2016

Dear sweet wonderful global family, how beautiful is the light! I once again sit here at my quiet little 37th floor perch totally engulfed in the magnificent beauty of thousands upon thousands of city lights, contrasted with the dark majesty of the ocean waves. In their heartbeat, I hear the reflection of a planet that embraces us all if we will but let it.

The pace of Schuyler's rehab has been fast and furious—joyously so, but leaving me few moments to connect with my dear global family—so I do apologize. Whereas in the ICU there were hours upon hours of pure focusing and projecting energy, in this phase, the WILL must be combined with the physical energy. I confess that I marvel in the fact that few of the "traditional" brain trauma symptoms have plagued us. At no point did Schuyler not recognize me nor did she appear to need an "anger phase" to regain her power. Schuyler is like a beautiful child in a petite but grown up body. She remembers so many crazy details and the neuropsychologists have said that she does not suffer from the normal "post traumatic amnesia". We laugh. We love. We look at the mountains in this recovery and plan how together we will savor the view…

Schuyler is talking up a storm. Her lip, tongue and vocal muscles get better every day so now even when she is exhausted, it is getting easier and easier to understand her. Monday, she was officially cleared to eat "mechanically soft" foods— meaning that some of her favorite foods like sashimi are back on the menu! My mornings and nights are typically spent preparing the next day's menu—green power smoothies laced with kale, turmeric root, goji, avocado, berries, banana, protein powder, Omega 3 as well as chopped smoked salmon, omelets, tabouli, desserts and much, much more. It's hard to express the joy that I feel when I see her ravenously eat!

Her muscle strength, coordination and balance are coming together little by little. She works tirelessly to relearn how simply to sit up for minutes upon end. She still cannot bear weight on her left leg so "normal" tasks like moving from the bed to the wheelchair become Olympian feats for my little one. Even when we fall on the bed in a "failed" attempt to transfer her to the wheel chair, we tend to collapse in laughter. She is learning. I am learning— and together we press forward.

What a journey! Absolutely everything needs to be relearned and requires Herculean effort and still quite a bit of assistance— from brushing her teeth to putting on a t-shirt. But throughout it all, we find time for as many glorious moments as we can capture! An excursion in full wheel chair regalia with wide brimmed straw hat and "movie star" sunglasses took us to the farmer's market on the hospital campus. For one magnificent hour, time stopped as we dined on freshly squeezed juices, smoothies, guacamole and tons of love.

Our appreciation of life must have been apparent because our hour was magical. We started that adventure accompanied by (yes!!) the EMT who had been part of the Air Ambulance team from Colombia to Miami. What an amazing man and part of such a special profession! To be able to hug him again and to show him our sweet Schuyler well on her way to recovery was a dream moment for sure! He came to visit us literally on his way to fly to Rome for a rescue that evening.

We found ourselves striking up numerous conversations with "random strangers" who were captivated by our story. We ran into one of the surgeons on the neurology team and he was obviously incredibly stunned by Schuyler's progress. Even the vendors could sense our joy and we found ourselves recipients of all sorts of yummy gifts. The sun was shining. The birds were singing. There could not have been a more brilliant moment and this adventure to the farmer's market became "one small memory" worthy of a lifetime!

The inpatient rehab time that insurance will cover is rapidly coming to an end, but I find myself feeling enthusiasm—not fear. We are waiting anxiously to hear if her ankle can start to bear weight and in a few more weeks, we see if the back brace can be shed. Little by little, she regains her physical strength. Inside this tiny body lies SUCH a will to live and to thrive! And in spite of the discomfort and frustration, she smiles and smiles and smiles. Even the nurses and the lunch lady refer to her as "Sunshine"!

Even with Schuyler's lightning progress, we realize that there will most likely be months of wheelchair time and outpatient therapy. Daunting, I suppose, but the blessings are far more numerous than the challenges. Feeling the love of so many adds a power beyond measure! Our family was always close but the rock that hit dear sweet Schuy managed to shatter any hints of distance that might have existed between us. My son and my oldest daughter have been the glue that completes this miracle. Saya with her infinite sweetness and all encompassing love… Linden with his beautiful balance of warmth and solidity. And my "new extended family": my new "sis" Amalita and the Estradas, the Tsavoussis family… too many of you in our new global family to name! New wonderful friendships from the ICU and rehab… so many wonderful people on this planet yet we walk by them every day without daring to reach out and to say hello.

Dear wonderful global family, we tread delicately on a tiny planet called Earth. We are surrounded with so much abundance and beauty. We are tickled and playfully teased by this thing called Life— urged to explore… urged to wonder... urged to create and to grow. We have but a mere century to savor and admire our individual paths. And although the beauty of our destination may be glorious, it is the joy that we discover ALONG the path that will define us and it is the flowers picked along the way that will give our experiences its beauty.

Look into the eyes of those strangers. Smile. Hug. Laugh. Live! BE the moment that you hope to see! Expect to find love. Expect to find beauty. There are many views of what it means to live on our planet, but each picture is but one picture and each of us gets to choose where we set our gaze.

So as I soak in the beauty of each brilliant light be it astral or man-made, I revel in the perfection of this great tapestry... Life is rich and great— a powerful gift for each to enjoy in his or her own way! Reach out there with your own special light and watch how quickly you can light up an entire city and quite possibly even the world! The Schuy IS the limit!

Much love,

Meridith

CHAPTER 13

The Next Chapter

Wednesday May 11, 2016

Hello, dear wondrous global family! May I share with you the flutter that I felt in my heart as I walked to the second bedroom in my apartment, slid the door open and peaked in to see our lovely warrior princess sleeping peacefully in "her" bed surrounded on the walls by cards, sunflowers, photos and limitless love? YES, Schuyler was officially discharged from Ryder Trauma Center Rehab on Wednesday after 2 previous "false starts"! We are now moving into the outpatient rehab portion of this adventure! How do I capture this emotion in mere words?

These past two days have been beyond magical. Magnificent. A hugely significant moment in this journey. And interestingly enough, the majesty of this experience has gone far beyond watching Schuyler stand unassisted for 30 seconds (although that vision brought me to tears) or cradling her from the wheelchair into our car for the journey home. Yes, as I sat here last night soaking in the gorgeous city lights, it struck me that an important yet unexpected "catch your breath" significance has been discovering all of the new life inspiring relationships that "tragedy" seems to inspire. The greatness in others is massive and the resilience of the human soul is immense.

So where do I start? Initially we were told the the insurance demanded that Schuyler be discharged last Friday against the wishes of the hospital staff. However, Schuyler developed a UTI with fever that prevented her discharge. Nevertheless (wow) what a Mother's Day! Schuy's brother and sister and sweetheart Jordan wheeled Schuy out to the picnic tables where I had set up a surprise spread of Whole Foods yumminess. Hummus. Sushi. Tabouli. Watermelon. Tarts. Orzo. So much more! Laughter. Hugs. Smiles. And the feeling that Life and Love couldn't be more vibrant!

Three more days of therapy and Schuyler was truly being pushed far beyond what looked to be her comfort zone. They had her kneeling up and down then lying down and pushing (so hard) back up. Next they had her attempt to stand— knees trying to buckle, legs shaking, torso swaying and eyes focused with all her will on that mirror. She WOULD stand! You can imagine my maternal gulp when Lourdes said, "Now Schuyler, I'm going to see if you can do it on your own..." Five seconds, ten seconds, fifteen seconds, THIRTY!!!! Back in the wheelchair—exhausted! I couldn't have been more excited and in awe. "Now, Schuyler, let's see if you can walk..." I just about gasped out loud in disbelief. My maternal heart feared that it was much too soon— and yet I had to let her try...! The gait belt goes on. The mirror gets moved farther away and Schuyler is once again pulled up out of the wheel chair into a standing position with that huge orthopedic boot still strapped onto her left foot. It was all that I could do to resist bursting into tears and running to her "rescue". This therapy certainly demanded my own brand of willpower and profound trust. I held back the tears and instead added my own words of encouragement to my baby warrior. My heart was pounding!

Out swung the right leg. The left knee started to buckle but Lourdes held tight. One step! The left foot swung out, crossing too far in front of the right…more wobbling…again Lourdes held tight. With pure unbridled determination, Schuyler clung to the walker achieving more and more small but mighty steps. I could barely breathe from the power of the avalanche of emotions that I was feeling. How tiny and fragile she looked yet this formidable challenge was not about to defeat her! My own job during this incredible process is to buoy her with love and to feed that unstoppable spirit.

On Tuesday, we got word that Schuyler's fever was gone and she was cleared for release on Wednesday. Her outpatient therapy would start the following week. Although we were excited beyond belief, the logistics were a bit daunting. In spite of Schuy's sister Saya's attempt to be here to assist me, it looked like the delay in the release date would mean that I would have to get Schuy and her gear back to the apartment by myself. Not impossible—but definitely intimidating. I have gotten surprisingly adept at "transferring" Schuyler from bed to wheelchair and from wheelchair to the car, but I have discovered just how soothing it is to have even one other human being there to cheer you on! And sometimes physically, it's just tremendously challenging to push a wheelchair and push a cart of belongings simultaneously!

At the last minute, true to form, my "behind the scenes angels" arranged for their two close friends to meet me at the hospital for the discharge. When they arrived, our belongings were literally loaded up on the hospital cart and I was getting ready to head over to the garage to grab my car. A favorite nurse was ready to bring Schuyler and gear down to the loading area. The timing could not have been more perfect! This wonderful couple swooped in and gave me an extra two pairs of hands to load the car. They even agreed to video tape our "grand exit"! The magical moment that we had dreamed of now for so many months had finally arrived!!

I ran to the garage to get my car. My "twin sis" Amalita began conferencing people in on my blue tooth. As I drove into the circle, the sight of "baby Schuy" there in her wheelchair with three guardian angels was euphoric! I rolled down the windows and everyone on the conference call began cheering!

Schuyler in her wide brimmed straw hat and leopard sunglasses looked every bit of a movie star— smiling her brightest smile! Our angel Santi began filming this moment as we began the load in! Like a crazy game of Jenga, we miraculously fit all of the gear into the Green Hornet (yes, I long ago insisted on naming my car). How extraordinarily delicious was the moment when I embraced dear sweet Schuyler and transferred her into the car! The car was thundering with the cheers of everyone on the blue tooth! I gave a HUGE HUG to dear Christianne, who had been such a special member of the rehab team and then ran to finally jump into the car and whisked dear sweet Schuyler away! Both she and I were absolutely BEAMING!

I had promised her a "break out lunch" at this trendy Peruvian/Japanese restaurant in Wynnwood called Suviche. Our angels Mercy and Santi were totally on board for this excursion. For the next two hours Schuyler reveled in the exquisiteness of each new moment— feeling the warmth and the breeze of the outdoor terrace, drinking from a "real" glass, sharing stories with amazing new friends and dining on phenomenal ceviche, tataki, sushi and caramel pie. Life could be challenging and still be DELICIOUS!

As the sun had set on Wednesday night and I brought Schuyler over to the window to look at the captivating lights of this city, I couldn't help but squeal! FIREWORKS—YES FIREWORKS ON A WEDNESDAY NIGHT positively exploding over South Beach! But of course! God Universe, you are amazing!

And so, dear global family, we begin the next chapter! Still many, many mountain peaks on this journey but the air is fresh and clean and the skies are infinitely blue! I have learned a lot on this path and I have met many people that take my breath away. There are definitely so very many people who are generous, loving and good. And by connecting our own goodness with the goodness of others, we create a vibrant force that is intensely powerful and far-reaching.

I have rediscovered my love of Life and of Humanity. I have learned to sometimes think INSIDE the box by TALKING to those other people in the elevator. It's amazing to see what happens. Smile, love, embrace and see the world change! Yesterday evening, I wheeled Schuyler down to the beach and we sat and watched the beauty of the infinite waves. We sang. We LIVED.

At times, each of us here on this ever-spinning planet may feel like tiny single individuals overwhelmed by "what is". But suppose we could instead focus our attention on the "what if's"? We are a species that has intentionally been given the power to dream and to imagine. And as the saying goes, "If your dreams don't scare you, they're not big enough". My dear wonderful global family, magic truly abounds. It doesn't lie "out there". Only through the magic within do we gain the strength to see the magic on the outside .

The most powerful magic lives within our hearts—within our souls—so beautifully connected with the God Universe that masters "the flow". We CAN be that miracle. We can banish the thoughts that no longer serve us. WE are meant to flourish and we are meant to live.

We are also meant to love and to love generously. Love explodes with infinite far-reaching power. Love is contagious. Love matters. Love DEFINES you. Love is the color in an otherwise black and white world...so LOVE WITH ALL OF YOUR HEART AND DRENCH THE WORLD IN YOUR POWERFUL SHINE!

As I said good night to the evening lights last night, I paused to bask in that one final moment of this landscape. Each light so uniquely powerful and delicious! And the visual masterpiece that was created by the joining together of all these individual lights into one breathtaking city! Captivating!

Today, let's BE the city! Let's join our lights with the radiance of those around us! Let us shine brightly and add dazzle to even the darkest sky. We are ALIVE and meant to be exactly where we are right now and there is a world full of elevators with "strangers" just waiting to be talked to….

It's nap time here on the 37th floor and I pause once more to soak in the vision of my sweet global daughter sleeping blissfully on her own special bed…Miracles do happen! The Schuy is the Limit!

Much love,

Meridith (and now Schuy!!!)

May 21, 2016

Hello, dear embraceable global family! GOOSEBUMPS!! The vision of sweet Schuyler curled up last night on the couch surrounded by our furry family (Tinkerbell and Frodo) and doing brain games with my mom left me gasping in awe. Thursday, marked the three month mark after the accident and the world has given us more miracles than one would expect in an entire lifetime! Barely five weeks ago, my sweet child was lying in a hospital bed unable to sit up and communicating only by hand squeezes. How far we have come— and how glorious will be our steps ahead!

Tuesday was the first day of outpatient rehab. I confess that I actually overslept so it took all of my determination to get on the back brace (aka "the shield"), get on the left foot boot, dress her, sit her up, transfer her to the wheel chair, wheel the chair into the bathroom, transfer her to the toilet, transfer her back to the chair, brush teeth, wash her face, wheel the chair to the kitchen table, give her the one medication that must be taken 30 minutes prior to eating, whip up a smoothie, heat up the omelet that I had cooked the night before, bake the toast, butter the toast, cut the toast, feed her all of these delicacies plus some greek yogurt, give her the rest of the morning meds and zoom out the door in 52 minutes flat. Normally, this takes us about an hour and a half. Faint!

Imagine my delight when I got to the hospital to discover that absolutely every one of my credit cards and ID had fallen out of my phone case and were vacationing somewhere in that 37th floor paradise back in Miami Beach... gasp! Normally that would have been a "game over/ go straight to jail" moment because the only golden ticket into the hospital is your photo ID. However, as tends to happen in our story, Schuyler's therapist "just happened" to be down in the lobby. (How is this even possible—but yes, it's true!) She whisked us beyond the security guard, connected me with the outpatient therapy in-take goddess and disappeared with Schuyler up to the 4th floor. My heart was pounding but I just had to smile...

As the mother/"caregiver", I confess that this phase in the recovery experience has been beyond immense. I look back and I think of one of my favorite members of the ICU team 6 weeks ago telling me that the rehab portion of this journey would be the toughest. It seemed hard to fathom at the time considering what I had already been through. He described it by saying that "you will be her Zen. It will be your strength and your energy that feeds her and keeps her going and you are already going to be so tired. Try to relax as much now as you can..."

There have been so many wonderful people who have crossed our paths during this process. The medical team in Colombia, the Air Ambulance team, the medical teams at both Jackson Memorial and Ryder Trauma — each and every one of these has been more wonderful than I could have possibly ever dreamed. They truly do become like treasured family with a very special bond.

We have also had such amazing support and generosity from all corners of the world (thank you, global family) and I have even discovered a "new sister" (love you Amalita) and a new "family" (Chris, Georgette, Alexis, Santi, Merci, Dana)...remarkable... and the fundraisers! I am humbled and appreciative beyond words!! The overwhelming generosity has inspired so many tears of joy and such a monumental feeling of true gratitude for human kindness!

Yes, as glorious as this all is, the day to day logistics still can some times be overwhelming as I try to juggle more things than I would have thought possible… yet even in this taxing phase there is profound greatness, beauty and discovery.

All too often, we let "what's happening to us" control our thoughts and feelings. We start to believe that we must have certain circumstances in order to feel joy and laughter. And suddenly, we have given those circumstances, events and behaviors the ultimate power over our hearts. Dear global family, if this journey has taught me nothing else, it has taught me to understand that circumstances DON'T determine my mood—I determine my mood! And when I look for reasons to make my heart soar (even in the tiniest moment), the world starts shifting to make good things happen. And when you look with a joyful heart there are powerfully uplifting things even within a crisis.

The God Universe is magnificent because there is an abundance of beauty and grace all around us and within us. Each blue sky, each baby's laugh, each purr of a kitten beckons us to smile... Each opportunity to love, to marvel, to savor, to bask.... God Universe whispers at us to remember to feel joy, because joy is the key to powerful creation!

Before something like Schuyler's accident "happens" to you, you don't really know how you will react. In my case, within days, I was fortunate to feel tightly embraced in a sense of "knowing" that Schuyler would be fine—whatever that new fine would mean. It was much more powerful than a belief because even a belief has cracks. My sense of knowing was airtight and invulnerable to doubt, to "reality" or to any other outcome.

As I look back, I continue to marvel at the beauty of that feeling. What I felt was an exquisite emotional tapestry of forgiveness, appreciation and unconditional love. Yes, certainly I was able to tap into my unwavering belief in the power of the God Universe's ability to create miracles. And yet, I don't believe that one can start "believing in miracles" or practicing "positive visualization" at the start of a crisis. Fortunately, it was a perspective that I have embraced (and studied) for years with a particular passion for the work of Abraham-Hicks.

There have definitely been other huge challenges in my life, great sorrows and tremendous frustrations. Throughout each of those, I had the opportunity to "practice" my beliefs, my faith and quite honestly my ability to deliberately focus my attention. In a world where we tend to let our thoughts flow as they will, it was an interesting exercise— sometimes more successful than others. And I found that for me, simply stating a positive affirmation sometimes made me more aware of the absence of that component than making me feel its presence.

For years, I wrestled with weaning myself from thoughts that no longer served me. Sometimes, I am infinitely more successful than others. Certain topics definitely come more naturally than others. Yet, I persisted and worked and worked and worked on my focus so that I could try to "learn" to genuinely "feel good". Just because the "reality" of my circumstances appeared to be "not good", I was not obligated to feel bad. I had to learn to really embrace with every ounce of belief and trust that I could muster that I could not "get it wrong"— that every step and stumble ultimately is leading me toward a great and luscious journey that will fulfill my soul, if I will but let it….

Today, dear global family, look for the fun in each and every moment. Create fun by smiling at strangers or giving that hug to the person who looks like they need one. Express your deepest affection and appreciation for those who are close to you! Deep within each of us lies the essence of a child waiting to come out and play— just as all around us lies the perfect playground waiting to be played upon. So remember that you were born to play!

Today, dance for no reason! Laugh with pure joy! "Listen" to the soul of each special moment! Spread your arms wide and embrace the Universe. Daydream with abandon of love, abundance and achievement! And savor all that it means to be YOU and to be gloriously alive!

We are all uniquely powerful and important with a special calling to fulfill. Listen to your heart, lie in a field of flowers and know that precisely because you are you, ANYTHING is possible! The Schuy is the Limit!

Much love,

Meridith

May 31, 2016

Hello dear beautiful global family! BIRTHDAY ALERT!! SOON TO BE 23!!! What a week AND WEEKEND we have had! How glorious it was to sit here on the balcony of "37th Heaven" with my darling Schuyler inside happily talking via FaceTime with my mom. And the party this weekend!!! So much joy! Such happy energy! A room full of love!!! Tomorrow— ok technically today, on the 31st, her actual 23rd birthday!!! Mambo!

Last Monday, we set the alarm for 6am so that I could walk the dogs, quickly shower and zip through Schuyler's morning routine in time to be out the door by 8:30! Bit by bit, I can feel Schuyler's strength growing. Transferring from the bed to the wheel chair involves making sure that both of her feet are flat on the floor then wrapping my arms around her with one hand grabbing the bottom of the back brace (i.e. "the shield"). I remind her to lean forward then I bend my legs and count to three. She pushes up and I push up and miraculously we both end up standing! Haha!

It's hard to describe that blissful feeling when she is there in my arms. It's a moment that is almost like a hybrid between the most indulgent hug and the perfect waltz. How long it had been since I had been able to get a full hug from this amazingly buoyant spirit and now these "in transit" luxurious hugs are part of the transferring process. Lots of hidden joy in among the labor!

This week, for the first time, I realized that Schuy's balance was improving so well that she could steady herself with her left hand on my shoulder and I could move my arms away from the shield. She stood that way for two full minutes several times throughout the day and my heart absolutely leapt in joy each time that she accomplished it!

On Monday when I transferred Schuyler into our trusty green Genesis (the "Green Hornet"), I just knew that this first follow-up doctor's appointment would go fabulously! And indeed it did! Final x-rays of her spine were taken and our wonderful Dr. Wang proclaimed that he had an early birthday present for Schuyler: no more need for "the shield"! He suggested that Schuyler might need to wean off of it gradually, but even in this still fragile state, Schuyler was willing to risk a few sore muscles if it meant finally feeling the lovely sensation of having her torso FREE for the first time in months!! And the x-rays—oh my! Schuyler definitely has a few metal "embellishments" in her little 107 pound body! But onward toward wellness we go!

Another early morning on Tuesday as we dashed to catch Schuyler's therapy sessions that began at 9am. More intense work on her upper torso balance and strength! She is now able to sit supporting her own weight for longer and longer periods. She can hold her balance when the therapists try to push against her. More practicing getting in and out of the wheelchair…. more standing… more baby steps between the parallel bars….

On Wednesday, Schuyler and I spent the day at home. It's pretty much a non-stop day of transferring Schuyler from bed to wheelchair and from wheelchair to toilet and from toilet to wheelchair and from wheelchair to sofa and from sofa to wheelchair and from wheelchair to toilet and from toilet to bed and from bed to wheelchair… you get the picture. There are meals to be prepared then meals to be served. Schuyler's right arm is still too weak to lift more than a couple of inches so she needs help getting that arm into a position where she can get a fork or spoon to her mouth. Her left arm is much more coordinated and strong so this dear child might come out of this being ambidextrous! It wouldn't surprise us at all! It's a learning experience for her and also a learning experience for me! But the exhilaration of the consistent progress takes my breath away!

Wednesday evening, we had a physical therapist actually come work with Schuy in our apartment. (Thanks to all of you who donated to our fund. YOU made this possible.) The insurance company only covers 35 visits to therapy and Schuyler still has many physical challenges to overcome before she can really attempt to perform any "normal" activities safely on her own. The independent home therapist Arlene is a wonderful addition to Schuy's hospital rehab angels. Both Schuy and I loved her instantly!

Arlene actually had Schuyler up on her feet, hands against the sliding glass doors, taking small lateral steps as Arlene held her. She repeated the exercise again at the back of the couch. I can't tell you how exciting it is to see "Baby Schuyler" starting to stand in something that resembles her pre-Colombia posture! When she worked with Schuy again on Friday, she even had Schuy on the ground on her stomach doing baby versions of a hover/plank! I couldn't believe what I was seeing! How many, many times that I rejoice and marvel during each day!

On Thursday, more cause for celebration! This time, we headed off to the orthopedic team's offices. How exciting it was to see the look on those surgeons' faces when they saw Schuy's progress! Some of them had not seen Schuyler since she was released from the ICU! To have her talking and smiling and laughing in her little red flowered sun dress with wide brimmed straw hat obviously was a highlight of their day. This sort of miracle is most definitely why they do what they do! More x-rays and a huge "yay" when the doctor said that Schuy no longer had to wear "the boot"! The bones in both scapulas, upper right thigh and left ankle are officially healed!

To see the volume of screws, rods and metal inside our little maiden warrior makes one thank God for modern medicine and the dedication of these amazing medical teams! Wow! The airport security will definitely get to know Schuyler!

So, off came the boot! Shoes and socks were ceremoniously adorned onto both of those beautiful feet then we were off to the Farmer's Market on campus for lunch before therapy. It was a gorgeously delicious day in Miami with a balmy breeze and big, poofy clouds floating leisurely through the blue sky over the grassy quad. The ladies at the Peruvian stand remembered Schuyler and once again gifted her a fruit juice medley. The taste of those nectars was pure liquid paradise, but seeing Schuyler hold the cup in her dainty left hand and now drink that delectable liquid on her own was better still!

It was the perfect afternoon "picnic": ceviche, avocado, a custom "healthy juice" concoction, fresh fruit mélange featuring kiwi, berries, papaya, pineapple and melon, and a lovely Peruvian dish featuring seasoned chilled potatoes that were "mashed" around a lovely shrimp salad! Pure heaven!

Up we went for Schuy's afternoon therapy. As she started her occupational therapy, I scooted down to the pharmacy building to pick up some missing medications. When I got back up to Schuy's therapy, they told me that they were going to take her to aquatic therapy in a couple of weeks! So much to look forward to! I just had to grin and hug her as they wheeled her over to once again tackle the parallel bars and "tiny stepping".

On Friday, friends and family began arriving to celebrate Schuy's birthday on the 31st! The magnitude of such joy, love and appreciation was powerful indeed.

On Saturday, it was all about Schuyler! By 7:30pm the room was filled with dear friends old and new. Music graced the roar of the oceans below. Laughter resounded from corner to corner. Smiles, hugs, well-being and love presided. Schuyler could not have looked happier, nor could we. No one dreamed last year at this time that this is where we would be, but we are better people from having walked through this valley. We have truly LIVED and expanded.

Tomorrow is Schuyler's birthday and needless to say, to have her beside me cooing, laughing, "shoulder dancing" is the ultimate gift to me and to every one of us in our family! Her gorgeous little left eye so wide and full of wonder melts my heart to no end! Her right eye just starting to open...Her beautiful smile! Her infectious laugh— all are such HUGE rewards for the challenges that I face in this journey.

Yes, dear global family, I won't pretend that this doesn't require tremendous courage on my part as well as on Schuy's. As you might have guessed, when something like this occurs, you have to jump in with both feet and put virtually every other aspect of your life on hold— your source of income, your relationships, your routines.... Ironically, it's not actually Schuy and her progress that demands that I be courageous. The work right now is definitely physically exhausting yet being part of her progress is exhilarating to no end! Caring for Schuyler in this phase of the journey is a full time joy as much as it is a full time job. There are so many moments that absolutely leave me feeling like I am blessed to be living this!

The scary novelty of so much responsibility and pressure has relaxed into simply a very busy new routine. Amazing how we do adjust. There have been broken blenders and shattered glass, soiled sheets and endless wrestles with velcro. And the laundry—oh my gosh, the laundry! Yet, in the midst of tons of appointments and "must-do's", we find time to live. Adventures down to the beach, birthday cake shopping at Whole Foods (with one of the sweetest guys behind the counter), mother-daughter hour at Lincoln Road Doraku sushi…. it's all part of this crazy magical experience that weaves the richness into the tapestry of our lives. We grow and we live in full Dolby sound and technicolor. We in some cases must "fight" to be happy. It can be far too tempting at times to focus on the challenges.

I have heard that the word "courage" originates from the word "coeur" which in French means heart. Ironic because maybe the ultimate form of courage is to listen to your heart. And I mean to really listen… there are often things that we don't really want to hear— to the point where we fear hearing our heart say such things… and yet our heart is connected "bravely" and genuinely to the God

Universe that hears our most inner most dreams. Our heart knows where the "there" is that we want to go—even if we believe that our own road map is the shortest route. When our heart aligns with the God Universe we may believe that our lives are "falling apart" when in reality all the power of our being is "coming together" in the most awe-inspiring, grandest of ways!

Probably the toughest challenge for me personally has been the financial hit. This journey came during the three month window when my business generates about 80% of my annual revenue. Needless to say, it's tough to make cold calls from a busy ICU room or during rehab. I am the primary income generator so the hiccup that I am feeling is enough to definitely generate sincere fear. And yet there could have been no other path. My daughter NEEDED me and needs me still. This is the unconditional love of a parent. And even in the worry, there is a profound reverence.

My dear wonderful global family, there are times when all of us are going to face monumental challenges and unfathomable choices. There will be tears and there undoubtedly will be terror. And yet during these times lies an abundance of opportunity.

We are magnificent souls. We weep and we writhe in order to align with our true power. We crave growth and we binge on the concept of all encompassing happiness. We are free to choose. We are free to live. Our darkest hours come only when we feel alone and disconnected from all humanity or from the light that shines within us. So look for it with those "real-eyes" (realize) and embrace your own true strength and beauty. Run to those who will love you, embrace you, appreciate you and in some cases support you when you fall. Those who think that they are islands are destined to remain islands. Those who will share a vulnerable messy hair day hug with a new found friend are perhaps the heartbeat of all that could be.

This glorious God Universe has given us kittens and crazy chocolate dachshunds who lie on their backs without a care in the world. There are mountains. There are waves. There is genius. There is art. There is abundance at every twist and turn if we will see it. All we need to do is to add our own energy and love. But most of all there is the energy of true connection. This creates galaxies. This moves life forward.

Run to your hearts. Be "coeur-ageous". Define yourselves not by what you work but by what you live. Dream. Connect. Empower yourselves by empowering others. Look into each other's eyes and dare to love. Life is not a given but the path is bright even when you can only feel it.

We are not failures if we face times that make us very afraid. We are simply alive and in a poignant and important chapter along our journey. I believe that Life truly and sincerely wants us to "succeed" by finding our heart's desire. But success requires a "rocket fuel" level of momentum and that momentum is often only created by challenge.

It is as much the darkness that surrounds the beautiful lights of this cityscape of Miami that creates the perfection in this vision. Were it all bright, there would be no depth and grandeur. My dear glorious global family, we are all truly on a magnificent journey. We will cry. We will love and yet we will live. We cannot get it wrong. We cannot get it done. We are meant to keep living and living and living...for deeply yet simply within this living is the delicate yet wondrous "meaning of life". Yes, the Schuy is the Limit!

Much love,

Meridith (And Schuy and the Family)

CHAPTER 14

You Is Full

June 11, 2016

Hello dear "embraceable you" global family! Such a magnificent world! And what an AMAZING week to report!! Yes, we are happy to share our FIRST FORMAL PHOTO OF DEAR SCHUYLER on her road to recovery! Our little warrior princess has not lost her sparkle even in the midst of her "fiercest battle"!

Here I am at what feels like the pinnacle of the world right now—bathing in the kaleidoscope of colorful lights that adorns this succulent Miami/Ocean/Sky landscape. Wow! The power of this Universe! And the roar of the waves…hypnotic, soothing and profound…. The wind and rain up here on the 37th floor carry the hint of impending storms so there is a dangerous grandeur in what normally would be a simple breeze…so intoxicating that I cannot seem to pull away…. how I will miss this spiritual haven when I return to Tampa!

YES, what an exhilarating few weeks it has been! Schuyler has spent almost the entire last 14 days reveling in her

23rd birthday surrounded by so many dear friends! To see her tiny face sparkle with such bliss has been beauty beyond words. So much love, so much joy… so many, many reasons to celebrate life and the deep complex beauty of the human soul.

Schuyler's friends have begun visiting and FaceTiming now on a regular basis. Whoever believes that Millennials are a self-absorbed generation needs to visit our 37th Heaven and see these kids in action. Schuyler's sister Saya has of course been at our side every single weekend since she and I journeyed to Colombia. Within moments of walking through the door, she cheerfully dives in and helps with each day's laundry, mopping, feeding… she is truly unconditional in her love and her support of her sister and me! Pinch yourself, folks: Saya actually LOOKS for things that need to be done! How lucky I am to be the mother of these amazing young women!

My son Linden, his girlfriend Jordan and Saya's fiancé Robert all come down to give us their support almost every weekend as well. Their laughter, love and wisdom lift us all up immeasurably! Schuyler looks forward to each and every visit with such glee. To see the wonderfully selfless devotion of the kids to their "baby sister" (and vice versa) absolutely melts my heart and makes each weekend a total blessing. Life doesn't get much sweeter than having the kids all crashed on the couch watching Full House 2 while I'm basking in the Miami Beach skyline out on the balcony surrounded by the glow of candles and the hum of life below. Yes, this experience isn't about "returning to normal"— not at all. This is about opening our eyes, hearts and minds so that we can create an even better normal than we ever dreamed about before. With each step of this journey, we are all learning and expanding in our own lives as Schuyler recreates her own.

Throughout it all, there is the ever beckoning call from the Universe to celebrate these moments—and cherish them we do!

Yes—though the temptation to focus on the challenges could potentially be great, the magnitude of all the love and support that surrounds us creates one mood and one mood only: one of divine APPRECIATION! Schuyler's friends Ahkeyah, Katie and Stephanie kept Schuyler enthralled in total giggles and snuggles during the weekend prior to Schuy's birthday. Dear amazing Forrest also visited for several days and during the entire time he too never stopped looking for ways to help! Whether it was lugging the recycling down to the 3rd floor (without me even having to ask) or pulling Schuyler's wheelchair through the sand so that sweet Schuy could experience the beach, he was always keeping his eyes open for ways to make our lives wonderful! How humbling to have so many friends traveling from all over the country to give Schuyler their love!

The following weekend, Adam arrived with his wonderful wide smile. He is of course always so supportive and loving to our baby girl! While studying here in Miami, Allie Rivera has been making sure that Schuy gets a healthy, steady dose of her favorite "romcoms" and hugs. The lovely and powerful Brontë also came for several days bearing numerous shades of nail polish, prayer flags, Native American smudges and the willingness to do everything from walking the dogs to pushing the wheelchair behind Schuyler as Schuy tackled her walking exercises in therapy. Yes, WALKING!!! (But more on that later....wink!) I confess that I truly missed sweet Brontë when she finally had to head home! Each of Schuy's friends is such a treasure!

There have been so many magical moments in the past two weeks days that

I can't begin to mention them all— or thank all of you who consistently reach out just to send us your support! And each day, we press on through the beauty of our challenges to embrace a new set of successes, a new repertoire of miracles…yes, seeing Schuyler muster all of her strength and developing balance to tackle the walker with her wonderful therapist Arlene made Brontë and I absolutely tear up. Once again, since she can't yet stand on her own, walking longer distances is not something that I would have expected that she could do. Yet, obviously, "can't" is definitely not a word in Schuyler's vocabulary.

As you can imagine, when Arlene first suggested it, my heart was pounding. I can only imagine how Schuyler felt! Out we went into the long, fashionably carpeted hall outside our apartment. The chic gray walls suddenly seemed quite daunting. Why was I suddenly thinking of the Shining—oh my! Nervous? Blush— maybe just a smidge. The bright red gait belt went around Schuyler's waist and Arlene helped Schuyler "lean forward to stand up". Carefully, Arlene positioned Schuyler's hands on the walker and braced herself next to Schuyler with one hand on the walker and the other around Schuy's waist.

On Thursday, Schuy's steps were flailing. She would kick her right leg forward and it would land in the path of the left foot. Arlene would coach Schuyler to move her right foot into the correct lane. Schuy would adjust by wiggling her foot over. There would be a brief wobble in her hips and perhaps a semi-buckle to one knee, but Arlene never let Schuy fall. I'm not sure whether I fully exhaled at any point during this process, but a mom's maternal instinct runs deep! Calm, mama, calm.....! And yet...parallel to my nerves was a HUGE sense of excitement! To see Schuy make so much dramatic progress in such a relatively short time was on par with winning our own personal Super Bowl! I stayed quiet so that she could focus but you can be sure that I felt like whooping into Schuy's famous victory pose!

Down the hall we went. Carefully turn, turn, turn the walker so that Schuyler could navigate the corner. A tremendously long hall lay ahead. Oh my gosh... my heart was pounding...Step, feel for her balance, move the walker, feel for her balance, step, feel for her balance, then do it again...and again... and again. It was all that I could do to stay silent and not reach for her when she would stumble. The amount of effort required was formidable so Arlene and I let Schuyler concentrate in silence.

Before we knew it, Schuyler had made it all the way to the elevators, requiring no break. The constant click click click of the elevators resonated like a metronome keeping track of all of our racing heartbeats. Having reached "the target", Schuyler finally stood and "rested" a bit, shoulders drooping and arms holding onto the walker for what seemed like dear life. Surely Arlene would ask for the wheelchair. She did not. Instead, she turned Schuyler back around toward the direction of our apartment and asked Schuyler what she wanted to do. Schuyler said that she was ready to begin again! I'm sure that the look on my face was a frozen combination of nervousness, awe and pure disbelief. Yet if she said that she could do it, I could certainly be there cheering her on! Let's do this!

Schuyler took the first step on the journey back to our apartment. She was obviously exhausted. Arlene held her firmly. She would not let her fail. More wavering. A couple more moments when her knees would buckle or her body would lean off balance, but Schuy persisted. Right leg, walker, left leg, walker, the new mantra of the 37th floor. On and on they went with me behind them channeling all of my nervousness into that little black wheelchair. Wow!

Such a moment! Back to the turn in the hall. Oh my gosh—please don't fall. More careful maneuvering. Oops! Legs crossed. Correct. Slight shuffle. Breathe. Yes, Schuyler managed to overcome all fatigue and make it all the way back to our door. Arlene counted and we had covered 134 feet! I can't tell you how excited all three of us were! We were hugging and laughing. Arlene just couldn't believe it! I was so excited! Schuyler let out a blissful "yay!"

On Friday, Arlene took Schuy out into the hallway yet again. This time Brontë was here. She offered to follow with the wheel chair while Arlene and Schuyler embarked on yet another session of walking with the walker. I attended to a few much needed errands before following them out into the hallway. I didn't feel like they had been gone long but when I opened the door, I didn't even hear them— much less see them. I turned the corner and they were unbelievably no where to be seen.

Although I couldn't imagine that they could have possibly gotten that far, I continued to walk to the far side of the long, LONG hallway, past the first set of elevators and my jaw literally dropped when I found them around the far corner making their way back from the furtherest part of the 37th floor! Schuy was obviously beyond exhausted at this point, yet she refused the option to stop and rest. Step, adjust, move the walker, adjust, step, adjust, knee buckle, realign, breath, start again, "keep that right foot in its lane, Schuyler", pause, start again… one step at a time Schuyler managed to blow Thursday's record out of the water by covering 233 feet by the time that she was back at our door! Monumental! We all were ecstatic! One step at a time, we bask in this glorious, profound process!

As magnificent as Friday was, Saturday morning was beyond special. Saturday marked the first time that Schuyler went back into the ocean since her trip to Colombia! Yes, THE PHOTO!

This wonderful foundation called the Sabrina Cohen Foundation was featuring the soft launch of their new "wheelchair friendly" bi-weekly beach event called "Sabrina's Beach". Not only did they make access to the beach available to wheelchairs, but they had these marvelous water wheels that looked like souped up chaise lounge chairs with pontoons attached to the sides and gigantic rolling wheels to navigate over the sand. The perfect way for those who are wheelchair bound to get in and surf the tide!

It was a glorious afternoon! The sun and the breeze were perfect! We wheeled Schuyler triumphantly down the beach path to the entrance at Collins and 65th street. Schuyler immediately was greeted with hugs and "paparazzi". Her bubbly euphoric attitude definitely endeared her to the attendees right away. Who can resist that powerful little smile! Photographers were everywhere and we hear that her photo was even featured in Sunday's Miami Herald. Who knows? That wouldn't surprise me!

She needed some time to boost her courage so initially we all retreated to the beach areas. The organizers had a wonderful array of healthy wraps, fresh fruit, pastries and beverages and the mood was incredibly vibrant. Laughter danced alongside the waves and the world felt profoundly kind and generous. After about 20 minutes of relaxing under the tents, Schuyler decided that she was ready to launch onto one of the Water Wheels! Oh my! We just KNEW that what we were about to experience would be like riding on a spiritual Unicorn— something that one typically experiences only in one's wildest dreams. Yet here was the gift of our reality: Schuyler would once again dance among the waves of this gorgeous Atlantic ocean!

The ocean in Miami Beach is pretty much impossible to resist. The water is a clear aqua that just begs to be explored and experienced. The waves are majestic and strong and the horizon is dotted with a vibrant array of cruise ships, yachts, cargo ships and sea planes. The beaches are relatively sparsely populated but those that are here laugh, play, savor... this is definitely a place that resonates human happiness!

Schuyler was psyched and ready to head into the water! Schuy's OT therapist Carlee, who had invited us to that event, immediately volunteered to help get Schuyler into the water wheels contraption. The sand makes transferring her from the wheel chair a bit trickier but Carlee managed it effortlessly. Schuyler was in the "magical floating chair" and all poised to hit the waves! Four of the volunteers including Carlee and her boyfriend wheeled Schuyler down to the edge of the shore. She was nervous but nevertheless thrilled. Into the frothy waves they took her, with all of the rest of us enthusiastically in tow. This was a dream moment for sure! The water wheels began to float!

With Schuy's feet secured under a protective strap, we all made our way out into the ocean waves. Crash would come a wave! We'd all squeal and laugh. Carlee and team would hold Schuyler securely in this wonder vessel. Up and down we bobbed and jumped and splashed! Bam—one wave would come! Schuyler would lurch and squeal in excited delight. Wait… wait.. bam… another! On and on went these moments of extended joy… smiles and smiles and the occasional salt water blast to the face… this first adventure evolved into 30 minutes of sheer watery bliss!

Schuy's excitement was infectious to everyone there at the event. She was so, so happy to be out in the water again and the thrill of riding the waves seemed to exhilarate her already euphoric spirit! She could not have been happier! And when I heard her respond to someone's "how are you" with the response "Life is good", I knew that this would be a day that I would relish forever! Yes, Life indeed IS good!

So, my dear darling global family, as I gaze out tonight upon this gloriously stormy night in Miami, I realize just how much beauty can lie woven within even the most turbulent weather. Tonight, the dense rain now manages to hide each and every one of the glorious lights of downtown Miami from view. Were you to be suddenly dropped onto our tiny planet to the spot where I now sit, you might never know that behind such darkness lies a breathtaking tapestry of millions of lights. And yet those lights are there waiting patiently to reveal themselves once again. Not unlike all of the joy and "miracles" that are waiting to be seen once we allow our own dark clouds to disperse.

So let the dark clouds go... yes, really...it's time to release the thoughts that do nothing to empower you. Instead, choose to dream and to live and to expect an entire CITY of lights to "magically appear" and to shine their lights for you— because shine they will. Shine they do and shine they will for ever more even when you can't physically see them.

Perhaps it's now time to rethink your perspective. What if all those "mistakes" were not mistakes at all? What if a catastrophe evolves into a blessing? What if you live so completely in each step along the way of your journey that you never actually "need" to reach your destination? What if those "negative experiences" were just "filling your tank" with the spiritual rocket fuel that you absolutely need if you hope to live your own infinitely full and enriching life?

What if the key to being a "useful", contributing member to our species lies within the word itself? YOU IS FULL= "you's full"/ useful. YOU IS LESS= "you's less"/ useless. In order to give back to this planet, you must live all that is you to the fullest! Deeply and completely with every ounce of energy and hope that you can muster! Yes, someone as tiny as Schuyler can impact thousands with her unbridled positivity and there is a hidden Schuyler within each one of us.

You, yes YOU, are so full of uniqueness that even the diversity of stars can't compete with your potential to shine. There is absolutely no one else on this gorgeous planet with your same infinitely unique collection of talent and perspective. You were intended to shine. Storms will come and storms will go because storms are an integral and DESIRABLE part of nature— even human nature. Without them we risk becoming a human desert.

So as you read our story, remember to live. Remember to love. Remember to connect, to laugh, to listen. Reach out— far out— sometimes beyond your comfort zone. Embrace each other. Embrace yourself. "Real eyes" all of the magic that surrounds you each and every moment. Expect miracles. Expect the best. Know that the YOU-IS-FULL you MATTERS. God Universe is counting on each and every one of us to explore our talents and dazzle the world with our gifts.

There is a luscious life out there waiting to be unleashed. So what if there is a storm or two or three or four? All the more puddles to splash in as you merrily dance, skip and hop along your way to eternity!

Run to your inner ocean! Celebrate and splash in a few waves. Find that inner space that reveals your own magnificent city scape and dream and dream and dream. It is not fairy dust to believe that believing leads to seeing. It is actually fairy dust to believe that the only way to recognize reality is to see it. Isn't today's "reality" simply the aftermath of what yesterday's dreamers have left behind… ?

So on we go questing for the answers to Life while playing in the ocean sand… maybe the magnificence of Life IS actually its questions.. like the dangling carrot, we chase it, but there is a definite sense of fulfillment when we learn to relax in the pursuit…

And the lights of this tiny planet burn brightly all the more magnificently in the deeper, darker parts of the night… it is truly the darkness that allows us to appreciate their beauty…yes, dear global family, we may never get "it" done but were it all completely done, there might be no reason for these lights to shine on… so shine on and on and on…remembering always the majesty of your own brilliance. Yes, dear family, we are all miraculous components of this magnificent creation called Life! And yes— The Schuy is the Limit! Or should I say limitless when you deliberately choose to believe!

Much Love,

Meridith (And Schuy and Fam)

CHAPTER 15

The Miracle of Change

June 23, 2016 ·

Hello dear glorious global family! Soaking in one of my last nights in this 37th Heaven! Yes, it's official: we are RETURNING TO TAMPA in a little more than a week! My heart is pounding! The Miami skies have been putting on quite a farewell show these past few days! Daily storms now boom their way across the Miami landscape hurling spear upon spears of monolithic lightning in their wake! Saturday evening saw whirling winds so monumental in power that the gales actually picked up a wicker couch from a 10th floor balcony and deposited it across the pool, over the beach huts, across the path, across the dunes, across the beach and into the crest of the waves. Looks like Mother Nature Miami is throwing quite the tantrum about our decision to return to Tampa... wink! Separation anxiety already! Ha ha! I feel your pain!

Yes, every day now we hear the roar of thunder and the faint scent of the distant rain. The swoosh of the car tires on the wet roadways adds a sensual pulse to the majesty of this balcony. How I will miss this magical perch on the cusp of heaven! Miami, you have grown on me in ways that I would never have imagined! Yes, I confess that I have definitely fallen in love with this energizing metropolis and it's a wee bit bittersweet to leave…!

Another magical week with Schuyler…truly! It does feel like we are always, always DASHING. The alarm goes off at 6-6:30am so that I can get sweet Schuyler to her first therapy sessions at 9am. I race the dogs out to the beach in back of this glorious condo building before I wake up the sleeping warrior. The sunrise is always amazing and I confess that it's well worth sacrificing the extra 15 minutes of sleep to start my mornings with a meditation on the beach!

Much to my surprise, I have grown powerfully attached to the Atlantic Ocean. Its sparkling clear turquoise waters and luxurious temperatures have won my heart! Now barely a day will pass when I won't steal away for a few minutes of "wave worship" from the shore or to actually immerse myself in its glory and to feel the power of these majestic waves against my body. It is an idyllic way to recharge my spirit and replenish my energy.

Saturday was another day when Schuyler got to play in the waves. Unlike the previous Saturday event, the ocean this time was calm. Beautifully and pristinely calm— and in spite of her reputation for being a thrill seeker, Schuyler admitted that the gentle rocking on the water wheels was a welcome respite indeed. She was in heaven. Big smile. Big elated sigh. Big moment of "giving in" to this wee bit of aquatic luxury.

Sabrina Cohen with her Sabrina's Beach concept is nothing short of amazing. She is a perfect example of how something "challenging" can transform into something life changing for so many. For Schuyler, it was the opportunity to savor an experience that was reminiscent of much that she loves— the tickle of a sandy beach upon her toes, the exhilaration of the waves, the abandon of an ocean that "controls" a major portion of Man's beloved Earth…. In each bob of a wave, it seemed like she could "feel" the day when she will once again swim unassisted. For almost an hour, she lay back in the water wheel vehicle and breathed in each delicious moment.

For many of the other attendees, this organization gave them a glimpse of life that can only be called profound. Unlike Schuyler, most who were attending will probably never walk again. Most had not been in the ocean for years and years. To watch them laugh and joke and truly experience this ocean was humbling and joyous beyond measure. Through this journey I have learned not only how much we take for granted but how frequently we go through life unaware of our power to enhance the joy factor of others. Whether it's helping to facilitate a project like Sabrina's Beach or simply reaching out to embrace someone in need, we DO have the ability to become catalysts for positive change. Smiles are contagious. Laughter is contagious. The power of Belief is the root force of all creation. Let us never forget or undervalue the immense potential of one "tiny" individual to inspire change.

Several of the therapists from Schuyler's program at Ryder were there at the beach donating their time. Over and over again, they would help to get someone out of a wheelchair into the water wheels. It typically took 4-6 people to push the wheel chair into the water and then those same people would chaperone the vessel as long as the occupant chose to stay in the water. What heroes! Carlee, Nathalie, Josie and all of you!

I absolutely REVELED in Schuy's joy. Whether she was out in the waves or napping under an umbrella, she was totally content. How rewarding! Yet on this day, it was an entire beach of joy! So many happy people! To see, for example, a young girl with a "go-pro" filming her father's first voyage into these waves? Truly magical indeed! These therapists obviously take such pleasure in creating successes for their fellow humans in need! Wow! Humanity at its best! I felt so soothed and at peace…

And Saturday was just ONE of our sublime days on this road to rebirth! Oh my gosh, yes! Our week has been FULL of jaw-dropping moments all rolled together at "warp speed" with a smile!

Schuyler and I actually got to paint TWICE at rehab! Some Miami artists donated their time and materials to the rehab patients at Ryder. Last week, we spent two glorious hours dipping in paints, shells, starfish and letting our imagination create masterpieces! Today again we painted. This time using masking tape to first tape out some geometric shapes prior to painting. The level of control in Schuyler's arm in just one week was noticeable! SO exciting!! It was so rewarding to see that all of our work is making an impact!

Art is such a vehicle for peace and healing. Schuyler's lovely hands and arms still do not have much strength or accurate control of their movement and yet the allure of this project removed any semblance of effort or difficulty. She may not yet be able to use a fork and a spoon by herself, but she can definitely create beauty with a brush!

Schuyler's sessions using the walker with Ben and Arlene continues to improve. Weight shift, weight shift, weight shift. Sounds so easy but feels so hard!

Play with balance. Listen, learn, try again, try again. What a process! As I work with Schuy during the day, I am very much aware that she is indeed "getting it". True, she is a far cry from doing anything independently just yet but the scent of that possibility is now closer than ever before. Our first true shower without assistance took place this morning! I woke up feeling poised and ready to conquer that! Give me a gait belt. Give me a shower bench plus a few towels and wash cloths and I was ready for the challenge! Clean never felt so magnificent!

Schuyler's final follow-up appointment with her neuro surgeon Dr. Bullock has now come and gone as well. It was another jam packed day that started early but the feedback was sweet! The CT scan shows that we are well on our way in the healing process. That one troublesome spot remains but her progress is beyond question. Dr. Bullock emphasized again what a miracle she is.

He took time to go over EVERYTHING—checking her eyes, her arms, her memory, anything and everything that would reflect upon her progress.

Schuyler's right eye has been slow to reopen so Dr. Bullock worked his magic and got us not one but two appointments with Bascom Palmer before we leave for Tampa! This clinic is ranked as the top eye institute in the world so we couldn't be more elated! We actually bumped into Dr. Bullock today at our final Jackson farmer's market (sigh) and had a chance to give him one last "thank you" hug! He actually called me the best mom ever... very touching and humbling coming from this great doctor...!

Each day now feels like a countdown. We have our regular "places and faces" where folks now recognize and seem to adore us... The special favors like the fourth free dessert from the wonderful folks at our favorite Japanese restaurant Doraku!... The smiles and hellos at Nespresso... The doormen, the valets, the security at the condo and at Jackson...the nurses, the doctors, the therapists (so amazing that they deserve their own shoutout in another update)... Miami has become yet another extended family for us. Truly a second home...!

And so Tampa here we come...! Therapy is already scheduled with the team at Tampa General! Woo hoo! Our return date is official! Time to say goodbye to this wonderful taste of paradise!

With the full moon above the water in Miami Beach, I marvel at Life and its beautiful mysteries. When I came to Miami, I arrived in the midst of formidable change. I had heard nothing flattering about Miami. I had no particular fondness for the ocean. I certainly couldn't really imagine me as a high-rise "urban" girl— and I tend to stay as far away from hospitals and modern medicine as can physically be managed. Boom! Welcome to instant change…

In a mere 4 months, I have learned to love all of the "conditions" that my previous beliefs suggested that I would hate. Staggeringly beautiful and awe inspiring! If one can be open, one might find reasons to love…

So, as I listen to the audible caress of the ocean waves, it strikes me that perhaps another lesson in the mix of this glorious journey is to embrace the power of unconditional love. It can be possible to love and laugh in the midst of conditions that you would not have chosen. So do we really need to have those perfect conditions in order to love? Does everything absolutely have to be under our control in order for us to relax and laugh? Our hearts and desires speak loudly to God Universe and it just might be that the "pathway" to our prayers lies down a road that initially might seem unappealing.

When these moments arise, how diligently can we continue to believe in "the process"? How tightly can we hold on to our faith? Do we trust this path and go boldly forward simply because our hearts say "Go!"?

Today, dear global family, I would urge you to celebrate the unknown. Look for the hidden gems. Have faith in the perfection of Change.

Focus on the greatness of the moment and of those around you— and you will find exactly that! Be one of the great ones for others! Jump on the bed! Toss around the pillows! Dance outside of your comfort zone and then body tango forward into what lies ahead.

Our time has come to change lives and to be all that we can be— as individuals... as a species! Embrace even the large boulders that come your way because sometimes that boulder is the key to living your own miracle! Schuyler and I have many, many dreams to embrace in the years ahead. In each of our own unique ways, we intend to give back to this lusciously wonderful planet. Dear global family, we invite you to join us! Live your moments with the intent to make your mark on Life! We CAN change this planet by empowering ourselves and then expanding to empowering others.

The challenges that we face are meant to help us grow and achieve— not to wound or to stop us. We are each "small but mighty" brightly shining lights. Put us all together and we light up the planet like this glorious 37th floor Schuy/sky. And shining brilliantly over all of our brightness lies the Mother Moon and her galaxy of stars! And for hours and hours during each and every night of each and every day, these lights made by Man join with the lights of the Heavens to create a dazzling masterpiece of glowing energy! Dear family, we are One and that oneness gives us the power of Many.

Believe in your path and open your heart to the magic that it is anxious to show you! We are not alone nor can our path lead us astray. The beauty of the journey is precisely because there can be NO DOUBT but that this journey will be an adventure to remember! The Schuy is the Limit!

Much love,

Meridith (and Schuy)

CHAPTER 16

Forests Must Burn

July 11, 2016 ·

So many thanks to Kera Mashek of WFTS for the lovely feature on Schuyler's return to Tampa. We continue to send our love and appreciation to each and every one of you who has supported us along this journey. We have a long road ahead but when surrounded by so many angels, we are far more blessed than we are challenged. All of our love and appreciation!

July 18, 2016 ·

Hello, dear global family! Yes, Schuyler and I are BACK IN TAMPA! Our final days in Miami were breathtaking…! The weekend before our departure featured a trip to Santi and Mercy's magazine worthy "farm house" on their avocado farm. My mother, my daughter Saya, her fiancé Robert, Schuyler and I were treated to a fairy tale brunch in the farm house of one's dreams complete with a lovely chapel on premise. This family is the embodiment of generosity, consideration, love and chivalry. Case in point, for this one meal, they actually built (and stained) a wheelchair ramp so that Schuyler could sit comfortably at their high dining table! Faint! Santi's one rule? That you make yourself at home and let them know how they could be of service… oh my goodness! We were truly pampered beyond measure. We were not allowed to wash one dish or even lift Schuy's wheelchair when it was time to depart. It was humbling, touching and inspiring beyond words… wow! We didn't want to leave! And we definitely have dear friends forever! Amazing souls!

On Tuesday, Schuy and I decided to make a goodbye visit to the ICU. We were hoping to give a final hug to Leo and those special nurses who had held Schuyler so near to their hearts. Schuyler has no real memory of the ICU so she was a mixture of curiosity and nerves.

Jackson has very tight security so I wasn't sure how we would get beyond the front desk but as the Universe would have it, my favorite security guard was at the desk. From Day 1, I have always chatted with the desk guards and tried to give their trying job a ray of sunshine. This guard quickly began recognizing me and over the passing weeks she too had become like family. With a huge grin and congratulations to Schuyler, she happily gave us a pass.

Onward we headed to the West Wing elevator and up we went. Understand that I don't recall ever crying while in the ICU. I know… sounds weird, but that's just how strong was my KNOWING that Schuy would survive. Yet, strangely, on Tuesday, as I hit the call button and listened to the doors finally swinging open, I was hit with a wave of emotion—like the sudden glimpse of understanding how close we had stood to a dramatically different ending. Joyous tears of profound appreciation and understanding. I wheeled Schuy through those double doors with my heart pounding. Her first tiny room was immediately to our right. I pointed it out gingerly, poignantly aware of the family currently within those walls. To my surprise, I didn't recognize any of the nurses—yet we had spent two months here. I took a huge gulp and pushed on. Suddenly, in the distance, I saw Hazel—one of the most significant nurses for Schuyler during her early days there. I pushed Schuy a bit faster with my eye on this dear woman, now with her back to us. "Hazel!" I cried out. She turned and for a brief moment she looked confused, then quickly registered my face. Once she recognized my face, her gaze turned down to the child in the wheelchair. "Schuyler?" she cried out! We all beamed, cried, embraced! Isn't this truly what life is all about?

Ironically, next to her, was the ICU "team" that included the doctor who had made the decision that one stressful evening to take Schuyler off all of her pain meds. In the ICU, the only way that they could communicate with Schuyler was by asking her to squeeze their hands for yes and for no. Schuyler had stopped responding to these requests so this doctor had to make a judgment call. This occurred during the beginning of the week following two weeks of back to back 10 hour+ surgeries complete with anesthesia so we ultimately discovered that Schuy was just too tired to respond.

This doctor remembered Schuyler well so when Hazel cried out, "Schuyler!", she immediately stopped communicating with her team and looked over. Now understand that in the neuro ICU, these teams are like the super bowl athletes: they have one goal and one goal only. Nothing upon nothing distracts them. They are focused on the game and the stakes are the highest.... and yet... everyone stopped upon seeing us... this doctor came over and said, "Schuyler?" She looked at me and asked if this was the girl who had been traveling in South America and who had a boulder drop on her body? When I said that it was, she literally dropped to her knees and stared at Schuyler as if she was seeing something akin to an intergalactic Unicorn. Impossible to digest based on the level of Schuy's injuries that she had seen!

In the meantime, another favorite nurse Sabrina had walked up. It was a magical moment in time… for a few brief moments, the solemnity of the neurological ICU gave way to the effusive awe of humanity embracing the undeniable solid evidence of the Miraculous. We smiled. We hugged. We catalogued this moment in a photograph. Apparently, few patients return to see these doctors and nurses because they equate their time in the ICU with pain and suffering. But to us, these human beings are the bridge to new beginnings. A special breed indeed! It was a humbling yet uplifting closure to the part of our journey that transpired in Miami.

The final day in therapy was emotional as well. One of Schuy's super talented PT therapists (We love you Ben) actually drew a phenomenal Schuy is the Limit card for her that everyone signed. They bought her a smoothie and did the final discharge evaluations. It was hard to believe that we were saying goodbye (for now) to the souls who had become so special in our lives.

Our last week included an amazing day of pampering courtesy of a new friend with her own magical story...Kim and her husband whisked Schuyler and I away to the posh Jade in Sunny Isles for an afternoon of mani/ped and massage. Gorgeous ocean views, wonderful conversation, luxurious lunch...what a treat! How glorious is life when we have the love of a global family!

Our farewell with our special home therapist Arlene was a tear jerker as well.

She has been such a champion with Schuyler. I will forever and ever envision her guiding Schuyler on her first steps up and down the halls of the 37th floor. From therapist to family! We are so lucky!

Goodbye to the Akoya... our group of special neighbors and the grounds crew...this truly now felt like home and I confess that it was very, very hard to leave it...

Even the ocean had a special farewell... I walked into the waves for what I knew would be the last time for a while— feeling overwhelming love for my new found friend the Ocean. The consistent pulse of the waves was soothing and at the same time powerfully playful... almost peacefully hypnotic yet energizing at the same time. The sounds caressed me. The moving sand below my feet synchronized with me. My gaze fell to a group of majestic pelicans— mesmerizing. I watched as this group of birds would glide overhead then torpedo head first into the ocean. From there they would just savor the rocking of the waves until they would all suddenly take flight and begin the whole process again.

I was mesmerized. I was possessed with a strong desire to get close to one of these incredible animals so I began gently making my way over closer to him. He sensed my intention and headed for the skies. No worries. I continued my worship of the waves. He landed once again to my right and began his float. I couldn't help but try to get closer... yet again. No luck. Off he flew once again and I couldn't help but remark out loud, "You silly one. You can feel me, can't you? All I want to do is to admire you up close just once before I have to go."

Well, that remarkable bird turned around, flew right over my head and nose-dived into the ocean directly beside me. It was such an immediate response to my request that I yelled out "thank you, Universe!" And together we floated for several delicious minutes—his eye peering firmly into mine— until at last I thanked the ocean for its lessons, strength and love. My friend the pelican left and with a huge smile on my face, I walked out of my ocean "home". As I ventured out of the waves, I turned and held my hands wide. Thank you, Miami ocean. I carry your strength with me forever. Your lessons are many. As a token of my love and appreciation, I bestowed upon the Miami ocean my own parting gift: one of my most beloved crystals, with abundant thanks and with the promise that I will become a messenger of the hope and strength that this ocean and God Universe inspired in me.

My son and boyfriend arrived on Wednesday to pack up the vehicles. Thanks to the help of Schuy's great friend Allie, her roommate Madison and of course wonderful Mirlan (courtesy once again of Amalita), we were packed up and (gulp) ready to go... On Thursday morning, the guys loaded up the vehicles and headed back to Tampa, puppies in tow.

Schuy and I shared our final dinner at the Pullman Hotel with one of the two Miami families that had been the first to embrace us in the ICU. Johanna and her fiancé and adorable son (as well as her parents and of course Stephanie) have been beacons of light throughout this entire Miami journey. Desiree, you were definitely another! Angels come in many, many forms so even though they may walk the Earth without their wings, you will know them by their smiles. These are definitely angels. We were blessed to have their hugs and love at our side!

...and then it was time to say farewell to Miami and be on to Tampa...

It was a morning of eye institute doctors and cat scans but ultimately our business in Miami was behind us and it came time to hop in the car and make that drive to Tampa....

A huge rainstorm ushered us onto Alligator Alley. It was as if Miami hated for us to leave…it was oddly scary to be saying goodbye to this city that we had grown to love but we knew that it was time… we pressed forward through the storm then suddenly the rain completely subsided. We were nervous—both of us— but we were on our way.

It was an easy ride. No stops until we decided that we really should grab some food. We landed at one of Schuyler's favorites: Pita's Republic with a franchise in Sarasota. Our order for a vegetarian island curry wrap quickly evolved into a wonderful chat about Life, Love and Belief with the man behind the counter. Peeling away at the layers of life… One step closer to Tampa….

Arriving in Tampa was a bit surreal. We got back to the townhouse and, were it not for my sweet child and the wheelchair, it was almost as if Miami and the accident had never happened. Even with a positive personality, change can feel daunting and at times overwhelming.

How to get Schuy into the townhouse? I became tremendously aware that our community is not set up to be wheelchair friendly. The curbs are high with only one slope at each end of the very long block. The garages are narrow and tight so if Joe's car is in the garage, there is no room for a wheelchair to pass by.

When we arrived, Joe wasn't home so at least I could pull my car into the middle of the garage and get her out without worrying about blocking the alleyway behind our building. I pulled the transporter chair out of the trunk, hung our "Mary Poppins" bag on the handlebars, hugged Schuyler up out of the car, did what I call the "high school slow dance" circle toward the chair then eased her into the wheelchair and headed toward the back door.

Schuyler and I banged and bumped our way through the garage. Many more obstacles and uneven edges than I had remembered or had been used to in Miami! Oh my! Breathe, Meridith. Breathe. I tilted the wheelchair up up the rather high lip, then there we were in the kitchen. We are here! "Home sweet home."

I took a moment to look around the room and soak it all in...the curtains that had been newly hung on February 18th (Still loving the look that they give this room...) ...The stair lift... The tight squeeze around and between furniture... Quite a few more challenges than I faced in the space in Miami, but it's going to be home... Keep breathing... Focus on this gorgeous child in the wheelchair and the two waggly tailed "fur-babies" who were obviously overjoyed to see us!

I dove into action getting Schuyler into the chairlift and upstairs for a nap. No big to do. No confetti. No marching band. No flowers. No banners. No hoopla. It was as if we had simply gone for a few minutes to Target. I felt a huge crunch and sense of panic and overwhelment but there was no turning around at this point. We were back in Tampa.

The chairlift is a Godsend to have in the townhouse but what used to be a quick wheel from living room to bedroom in Miami has now become quite the adventure! Stand Schuyler up and pivot transfer into the chair. Foot rest down. Scoot back. Buckle in. One segment up. A landing with a step. Schuyler has not done steps. Ok, let's make this work. Into a second chair lift. Foot rest down. Lean forward to scoot back. Buckle and ready to go. Run back down the steps, grab the wheel chair and muscle it all the way to the top while trying to avoid hitting the wall, hitting Schuyler or throwing out my back. Send the chair up. Turn the chair. Leg stand back up. Toes over nose. Stand. Back into the wheelchair and buckle her in. Another segment. Twisting and turning the wheelchair into a room with a bed that is ferociously high.

Ok, we have to learn to jump or prop her up or something…bumping into furniture… suddenly, far more challenges than we ever faced in Miami. I was also trying desperately not to think about all the bags upon bags upon bags of things that I must now sort through that now covered every spare inch of space in her room, my office and our closet. Where was everything that I need? And where do I now put things? I was using all of my deliberate intent to stay strong but the truth is that I was reeling!

Yes, definitely a different world than our Miami home, but we were back in Tampa which means that we ARE moving forward. I told myself to remember that I had expected this emotional pinch. I had known that this would be such a deviation from the routine that I had grown to love but I had to embrace this change and find a way to find peace within it. Breathe, shed the tears if you have to, but keep KNOWING that the calm positivity will return.

My dear, dear global family, change can be staggering no matter how positively you are wired and try as I might to look for the silver linings, it was obvious that ironically I would now be entering into a world of even more physical challenges. Yet this WAS the next step in our journey and we will not be overcome when we have come this far. Soon this will become the new normal. Soon I WOULD FEEL that delicious pivot when you know that you love your life and that all is well!

Welcoming Amalita, her husband Jaime and their daughter Valentina to the townhome for the first time that night was beyond amazing! Giving Joe the chance to get to know these amazing souls was so special! Seeing my lovely Saya's gorgeous smile as she walked into the door after her trek from Orlando was another heart flutter moment! Amalita and Saya were definitely determined to be my Friday Welcome Home Birthday Angels!

Amalita has of course become like a sister to me. She is always my champion and she is without a doubt a kindred positive spirit. To think that a mere few months ago, this phenomenal woman was unknown to me is hard to fathom! The gift of the new found family and friends will outlive any memory of hardship, I am certain! She and Saya were the calming waves in the midst of that transitional "storm" of change and our love for each other definitely steadied me as I regained my Tampa "sea legs"....

It goes without saying that my children never cease to amaze me. My son has blossomed into such a strong, solid rock. Even when we occasionally struggle on the "how" in this process, his goodness and love and desire to do the right thing shine through. His integrity and hard work— the constant long drives to Miami while juggling his own career's busy season! Wow! So humbled and proud! And that smile… leaves me breathless and pinching myself each time that I see it…

My daughter Saya is also magnificent beyond belief. She was in Tampa for the entire homecoming/birthday weekend with dear, sweet Robert supporting her/us all the way. Together, we swallowed these new logistical hurdles with a smile and a few extra beads of sweat. In the few moments of tears when the change seemed daunting, she was there with a hug and endless love. How is it that the ICU didn't shake me but that Tampa reduced me to tears? It's ok. It is really ok. Take a breath. Savor the good.

Pivot. Reconnect with your Self. You are not alone. You can do this. Give it a day or two… the reconnection will come…

I have never tried to hide my humanity from my children because I do believe that the power of Life is expressed in the beauty of both its ups and downs. And even I do at times feel the weight of the "formidable" and break down into tears. But it was my first weekend back in Tampa and my birthday weekend to boot so Saya was determined to make sure that I got a few moments to breathe and that I felt "birthday pampered". Roses, balloons, two special brunches, Saya made sure that I felt loved and appreciated! Watching the tenderness with which she loaded Schuy into the car and fed her, it was easy to see that she is devoted to Schuyler beyond measure—a true gem in my crown of emotional riches...yet another dream child among my many blessings. I started to inhale and breathe....

Our excursion to Amalita's farm over the weekend was glorious too! And of course the Universe couldn't resist inserting another giggle into the "coincidence" column: Saya was driving using her GPS because we of course had never been to Amalita's house prior to the Colombian challenge. As we drove up, I was stunned. I called out to the girls who were both in the front seat, "Tell me this is not Amalita's house…!" Yes, folks, Amalita's house is a property that has always caught my attention every time over the past decade that I drove this road. Of course it is!

Saya, Schuy and I were absolutely embraced by all four of "Mamalita's" wonderful children as well as her husband, Jaime. We shared stories over plates of greek salad. We toured the farm and showed Schuyler the kittens, the bunny and the horses. Amalita's touch was even present when my boyfriend Joe and I went to Bern's on Sunday. Amalita had two glasses of delicious Chardonnay waiting for us at our table and then made sure that they wrote "Happy Birthday, Meridith" around the plate of my dessert!

It made a superb meal with my wonderful boyfriend absolutely birthday perfect! What a special "sis" she has become… how beautiful are Life's ironies…

Schuy's Tampa therapy began in earnest last week. By Monday, her Tampa team of therapists was in place and things were really starting to look encouraging. They have several different "bells and whistles" that should help Schuyler continue to progress… a decibel app for the iPad, a treadmill with suspension belt so that she can practice walking, a wii to work on her balance… and another great team of smiling faces that will continue to widen the reach of our global family!

The weekend after my birthday was a weekend of Girl Power to say the least. Thankfully, my boyfriend endured the invasion and allowed us women to take over the sacred grounds of his townhome without a hint of complaining! Maria and Izzy arrived on Wednesday. Dana (yes

THE Dana) arrived on Thursday. Schuy's Pi Phi "little" Allie arrived on Friday with her PHENOMENAL family. Together, we adventured over to the fabulous Locale market/ restaurant in St. Pete, dined at the craft beer lover's haven "Tampa Bay Brewing Company" and enjoyed the most magnificent gourmet dinner cooked by Allie's moms "Faf" and Nancy. We met two of Nancy's wonderful friends while in St. Pete and laughed and hugged and laughed some more! Great wine. Great beer. Priceless company!

As I think of this weekend, I reflect that there have been so many, many heroes and angels along this journey for our family. From the phenomenally professional team of river guides lead by Olfer who choreographed Schuy's amazing rescue... to the mystery American tourist who helped the team get Schuy steadily up the incline to the river team's vehicle...to our new Colombian friends and host family... and of course the doctors both in Colombia and in the

United States, the air ambulance team, the nurses, technicians and rehab teams… friends like Chris, Georgette and of course Amalita (and the entire Estrada family) who have been our tireless champions from minute 1!

Our miraculous journey has seen friends like Alexis who took the initiative to set up the GoFundMe for Schuy's medical treatment (thank you again to all of you who gave so generously financially:

https://www.gofundme.com/ztq2n4r8/donate)

Friends like Tiffany and Izzy who set up a second GoFundMe to help now with the caregiver expenses while my ability to work has been so impacted (https://www.gofundme.com/schuyisthelimit)

The AMAZING members of our global family ("Mr. T", Belmora, NTDT, the Bravelets, the Yale Dance-a-thon crew, the NYC fundraiser, the t-shirts and more..) who set up the fundraisers and all of you who made them successful!...All of you who have organized prayers and Novenas for our special girl...Friends like Santi and Mercy who came to our rescue on Discharge Day...Desiree who showered us all with love and endless goodies to help us through this...

I have to appreciate our friends in the media who have shared our story near and far...ALL THE MYRIAD of friends old and new who have visited us and shown us such love, help and support!.. and of course, those of you who faithfully follow our story and send us such love and encouragement! We are truly a blossoming global family with so much cause to celebrate!

Yes, dear ones, there WILL be challenges as we dance our way through Life—but that is not a sign of failure or abandonment. Yes, there will probably be tears and at time even hardship. Ironically, that is precisely the beauty of it all. In that exact moment when we ask God Universe "Why" is when we potentially let go enough to receive the answer. While we are kicking and screaming in protest is when our souls jump forward to new horizons. THAT dear friends is the magic. That is how all that is truly new and magnificent is created. From our hardship often comes our most significant creation. As much as we hate to admit, woven into each of our precipices are the elements of all that makes our species so magical and deep! We NEED the experiences that make us weep as much as we crave the moments that make us celebrate.

It is those moments that shake us to the core that hold the greatest potential to encourage us to expand! To create those miracles! The beauty of our lives would be one dimensional without all the questions, all the yearnings, all the desires to create something truly our own.... for this is all part of the glorious magnificence of the sifting process that draws us forward...

Remember, even the most majestic forests must occasionally burn in order to ultimately thrive. Yet, once the smoke has cleared, the trees do not mourn their loss. New life is quick to take hold. I believe that Nature is one of our greatest teachers— it gives us the profound hints that (if we will observe them) will give us insights into the greatest secrets of Life. And even happiness.

So as I walk through my day, I suppose that I could see a thousand reasons to cringe and complain. Many things that aren't done or that aren't done right... things that are blatantly wrong...things that hurt... things that are inconsiderate or insensitive....things that aren't fair or that I "don't deserve"... things that are beyond enough... things that make me want to pack up and leave (if I could figure out where to go—

because I do take myself with me wherever I go...)

But even as I feel these emotions, there is a marvelous Universe pulsing outside my door. The night sky, the stars... the extraordinary beasts of our planet... the ebb and flow of Life that is so easy to take for granted...that one flower that makes me say "Oh my...!"

Yes, dear ones, there are thoughts that don't serve us that somehow manage to dig deep inside our emotional veins. There are beliefs and expectations and even social programming that tangle us into a web. Yet, the escape key is within reach...

At some point we must desire to passionately look for the good... not yearn for the good because that emphasizes the absence of it... we must learn to smile at the stumbles of our species as we would smile at the stumbles of our two year old child learning to walk...

But most of all, we must embrace the power that each of us has to create good and love and, yes, meaning... which brings me back to beautiful Schuyler who has generated such love in so few years by her ability to ignite the best in so many people worldwide...

Each and every one of us has that Schuyler component in us... ready to run out and embrace the world...and the truth is that as formidable as Schuyler is, she could not "bring out" qualities in anyone that they did not already have in themselves.... so what is the lesson here...that when given the chance, we truly can LIVE BOLD... we can aspire to embody unbridled "joie de vivre"... we can ride our own version of an elephant and rappel down our own life's version of a waterfall... we can believe in our ability to impact change...we can dare to dream of a world that feels a wee bit better than it did a moment before..we can take a giant gulp and decide to unleash that special person that we have been hiding within....we can finally be a great parent to our precocious inner child...

Yes, dear global family, the joy of a roller coaster is typically measured by the intensity of its drop, so grab the handle of the front row and prepare to be delighted! Our lives can be the ultimate thrill ride that leaves our hearts joyously pounding! And you had better believe it: the Schuy is the Limit!

Much love,

Meridith, Schuy and Family

CHAPTER 17

Schuy is the Limit

July 31, 2016 ·

Hello dear embraceable global family! Welcome to the conclusion of our first month back in Tampa! What a whirlwind! Such a special evolution…! Schuyler is making massive progress in therapy as we adjust to our new Tampa routine. Yes, with a little bit of positive intent, it is totally possible to find happiness and stimulation in between the time on the treadmill, the plank exercises and the mandatory nap time!

Our weekdays are jam packed with speech, occupational and physical therapy three times a week. Each session spans 45 minutes and covers everything from breath support to hand eye coordination to 15 minutes on a suspension treadmill. It is quite the workout for the little warrior princess, but she tackles it with determination and a grin.

Twice a week, Amalita and I do aqua therapy with Schuy. This is a magical time. Using exercises that we learned in Miami as well as suggestions from Schuy's Tampa therapists, we spend a couple of hours in the pool. Not only do we use water weights and resistance exercises but we make sure that she spends some time floating. Ironically, floating is particularly good for improving upper body stability. Anything vaguely resembling the sacred nap time is great in Schuyler's book so she eagerly embraces the float time!

Pool time is followed by hair washing, showering and lunch on the lanai. Amalita loves to pamper us so these two days are always a particularly luscious time of our week. This past week, we added adaptive yoga into the mix. We found this angelic instructor who lead us through an uplifting session focused on butterflies and the warrior spirit within us. Schuyler's previous experience with yoga and dance built her flexibility and that is a quality that she definitely did not lose. After class, we spent a euphoric hour in an enchanting New Age shop laughing, hugging and discussing the magic of miracles and the amazing power of God Universe. With a brief pit stop in the neighboring natural market where we picked up our lunch delicacies, Amalita, Schuy and I were off to aqua therapy joined by Schuy's friend Dylan.

It is exciting to see the progress with not even one full month back in Tampa. Schuy's posture is definitely better. Her voice is a little bit stronger. Her torso control...steadily progressing... her leg control... definitely getting better...the therapists are genuinely excited. They actually mentioned to Amalita that we were the ideal patient and mom.

Such a fabulous compliment! I love knowing that they feel that we are giving it our best! It is certainly uncharted turf for us! On Friday, Schuyler actually tied a shoelace twice! Not possible merely two weeks earlier. My heart jumps in glee when I see these steady milestones!

Life is definitely a gift, my dear family! First is the gift of a beautifully "user friendly" universe in which our magnificent planet perfectly orbits this powerful sun. The majesty of this world...! Significant that it continues to expand and find ways to thrive throughout the centuries. Our oceans... our forests... the tiny plants that burst their way in between the solidity of the sidewalks... We don't have to worry about controlling gravity or the atmosphere... the sunrise or sunset...they are a powerful "given" in our list of "realities"— yet what a gift! And our own body's cells that adapt and strive to empower us regardless of the chaos that we throw upon them...And even in those cases when the body can't fully recover, the beauty of the mind can still be deep and rich and meaningful...

The party! The Welcome Home Schuyler / Happy Birthday Meridith party...wow! About 125 friends (possibly more) descended upon sweet Amalita's farm. It was the weekend when Forrest, Kara and Katie were also in town. Forrest and I became the whirlwind prep team. Amalita had ordered some wonderful South American delicacies. I had ordered some of Schuy's favorite Tampa foods from Taco Bus and Pita's Republic. Forrest and I (and then upon their arrival Kara and Katie) dove into creating multiple cheese platters, hummus platters, fruit platters, salads and shrimp...fun bonding in the kitchen for sure!

Schuyler spent the afternoon being fully pampered by the wonderful women at Belmora salon. It was so lovely for Saya and Schuyler to be able to thank these angels in person for sponsoring a fundraiser!

ABC Action News (WFTS) generously covered the party and gave a shout out not only for support for the "post hospital" fundraiser, but for potentially donated services that might benefit Schuyler. Kera is so wonderful. She and her team couldn't have been more wonderful to have in attendance.

The setting was Amalita's welcoming farm property in the Tarpon Springs area. A tent was set up in amongst the horse paddocks and outdoor cantina. Brimming with sparklie lights, flowers and laughter, it was a magical evening— the embodiment of what this global family has come to mean to us. There we all were... a collection of beautiful souls united by this series of miracles... from some of Schuy's closest friends to those who had only become close as part of the blessing of this journey. It was awe inspiring and dramatically humbling to feel such love and support.

Schuyler received more hugs and joyous tears on that evening than we could count. We took her for brief respites into the house periodically so that she could catch her breath, but most of the night she was out among friends and family smiling a million smiles.

My dear global family, love is far more powerful than hate. Love can inspire great, great change even in the things that we believe to be unchangeable. Love dresses itself in joy and adorns itself with miracles. Love is believing the "I'm Possible". Love is trusting yourself enough to truly allow yourself to unfold. Believe in all that you are becoming. Believe that you do not need to "control" your life or the lives of others in order to truly live. Let it flow. Let Life splash up against you and dowse you with wonder. Be the Child in the Sprinkler of Life and get as wet as possible. You cannot get it wrong and you cannot run out of things to play with.

Find your joy. Find your passion. And giggle when that passion seems to mysteriously change… you are here to discover who you are and what it means to be totally and lusciously YOU! You are ALLOWED to be as fluid as water and as powerful as the wind.

Reach out with that Love energy and connect with your Universe. Just as there are stars that adorn the night sky, we humans are entrusted by God Universe to be stars of the planet. Some will shine brightly. Some may shoot across the sky. Yet each star is unique and important and part of the ever unfolding tapestry that we call Earth.

One tiny voice inspired by love CAN make a difference. Imagine the impact of millions of inspired voices! Join in that chorus!

The power to create miracles lies within each and every one of us. The only "secret" is simply developing the self discipline to believe that. Life is energy based so when you embrace your own unique joyous energy, you become a true force to be reckoned with~! "May the force be with YOU!" Now go be the Heroes of the Galaxy, dear family! The Schuy is the Limit!

Much Love,

Meridith, Schuy and our entire family

CHAPTER 18

Angels Raft on Water

March 16, 2016 (An Open Letter to the People of Colombia published in Colombian papers written by Meridith)

Dear Friends of Colombia:

I am the mother of the young woman who had the boulder fall on her body while vacationing in Colombia. It has been a whirlwind few weeks for my family but as Schuyler's treatment progresses, I could not go one more day without writing this letter to publicly acknowledge the true Colombian heroes who saved my daughter's life.

Schuyler's tragedy in Colombia is not so much a story of tragedy and mishap as it is the story of great miracle, great heroism and exceptional displays of human kindness and generosity. The host couple that took us into their home while we were in Soccorro, the extraordinary medical team that pulled Schuyler back from the precipice of death and of course the absolutely EXCEPTIONAL river guides who overcame all odds to get Schuyler back to Soccorro to receive medical help—- those will eternally be our "Colombian angels on Earth" when we look at this journey.

I have been told by doctor after doctor that the odds of Schuyler having survived her injuries are literally next to none. The most accomplished Emergency Medical Service workers in the US with all of the latest equipment would have been hard pressed to transport her from the accident site to the hospital while keeping her alive. I am told that at least 95% of all people who have the sort of lung injury that my daughter sustained die on site— not to mention the horrific injuries to her head and legs.

Fortunately for my family, the extraordinary guides of the rafting company not only kept their composure, but they organized the perfect rescue scenario that enabled Schuyler to be here today. Thanks to their foresight and advance safety measures, their company van was following along the route of the rafting group. When this calamity happened, these heroic guides sprung into action without hesitation. They calmed the other tourists and managed to get Schuyler up a very steep incline to the waiting van. According to the doctors here in the Miami ICU, had they not perfectly stabilized her during the ride over the unpaved road, she would have ended up paralyzed if not dead. Let me emphasize again that each and every doctor here in the US who has worked with Schuyler has used the word "miracle" to describe her survival. I absolutely could not have asked for more from this tour company.

I am convinced that had Schuyler not been fortunate enough to have this spectacular group of expert guides leading her journey that she would not be with us today. They behaved above and beyond what any mother could hope for and they are without a doubt some of the most awe-inspiring human "angels" in this miracle story of my daughter's survival.

But the work of these angels was not finished there. Once they had delivered Schuyler to the hospital, these guides stayed with Schuyler and her friend at the hospital. Even when I had arrived in Soccorro with

Schuyler's sister, at least one of them (but usually at least three or four from the company) was there on site to comfort us, bring us food and attend to our every need. On the day that we left Soccorro, they even drove the entire distance from Soccorro to Bucaramanga transporting our luggage so that Schuyler's sister could ride in the ambulance with Schuyler and with me. They left us with food for the plane and did not leave the airport until our plane was aloft. I will be forever grateful to them for their extraordinary heroism and kindness.

Yes, dear Colombians, this raft company was more than a blessing to our family and I thank God that they were with Schuyler when this tragedy struck. If ever there was a company to entrust with the lives of one's loved ones, it is this group of expert rafters.

The hospitality in Soccorro was something that I will share forever with other Americans. When Schuyler's sister and I arrived in Soccorro, we had no hotel reservations of course. The most charming and welcoming family immediately took us into their home. They stayed with us at the hospital and worked on our behalf since we do not speak Spanish. They fed us. They supported us. They made us feel like we were family. It was truly special — something that we aren't used to seeing back in the US. We will always hold a special place in our hearts for the people of Soccorro and for that family in particular.

And the medical team! How can I possibly thank these doctors? The American public's familiarity with the Colombian health system is virtually nonexistent and I think that most assume that Schuyler's chances of receiving modern medical attention there in Colombia were little to none. I tell you, my friends, this is absolutely not so. Even one of the top neurologists here in Miami complimented the work that had been done on site in Soccorro. The doctors in that small hospital of Manuel Beltran absolutely achieved miracles and saved the life of my daughter against all odds. Her injuries were beyond a doubt catastrophic and I will say again that more than one doctor here in the US has told me that patients rarely survive that level of trauma. And yet my Schuyler did!

Those doctors were invested in the survival of my daughter. They gave her absolutely the best care and attention that one could hope for. In many ways, they treated her almost like a daughter, reveling in each success and taking significant time to explain to us the potential challenges and to help us make the best decisions. And they did achieve a miracle: she survived so that we could get her back home.

People of Colombia, I know that most of us Americans don't yet know of all of the great and wonderful aspects of your country. So much publicity has been given to the negative. But let me say that I will do everything in my power to share our story and our experience. Colombia has been good to us— almost magical. The people that we encountered are some of the most extraordinarily good people that I have ever met. On behalf of my daughter Schuyler and my entire family, I thank you beyond measure! Please hold your heads high on behalf of the heroes of this story. Please treasure them for their extraordinary efforts and expertise. Colombia has much to be proud of! For this, we are eternally grateful! Thank you, Colombia!

Footnote to the Readers: It is my wish to one day (sooner rather than later) to be able to donate a portion of the proceeds from my Sky is the Limit pursuits to the ICU unit at Manuel Beltran hospital. Their dedication to Schuyler was massive. Would that I could some way continue to show my appreciation by helping other families in need!

CHAPTER 19

Greatness
Without Limits

Bonus Update November 8, 2017

Dear Sweet Global Family,

How far we have come together! Yesterday evening Schuy and I both had a good cry. Right there, in the booth in the middle of our favorite Tampa Japanese restaurant. X Ambassadors' "Hold Onto Me" (I'm A Little Unsteady) was playing in the background as we took a seat in one of the booths. Schuy looked at me and in her tiny little voice that still requires so much effort to be heard, she said, "This song reminds me of me... I'm going to cry..." I told her that I think of her every time that I hear this song. I told her that I'm sorry that things are still so hard for her and that if I could take some of it on myself, I would. "I will be right beside you all the way though, little one..."

As the singer crooned, "Mama... come here..." I felt that familiar lump in my throat and my eyes begin to fill with tears. My thoughts flashed back to that first moment in the Socorro ICU when Saya, Dana and I heard Schuy's "playlist". A tiny diamond-like tear rolled down from Schuy's lovely little left eye. We didn't say a word in that moment. We just looked at each other , held hands and quietly cried. Life's gifts certainly come in strange packages sometimes.

GREATNESS.

Greatness doesn't demand that you always feel strong… nor does it demand that you always feel joy. Greatness simply asks that you be YOU, powerfully, uniquely and whole-heartedly YOU.

Greatness resides proudly in the world of Uncertainty…the great Unknown.. full of adventure, full of expansion, full of promise, full of hope… Greatness demands that you find your own way… your own way to trust in this glorious process that we call Life. Greatness demands that you view your stumbles not as a fall, but simply a beautiful variation in the World's Greatest Dance.

Sometimes Life demands that we become reluctant heroes. I hope that when these moments come — and they will come — that you too will stand strong. And yes, believe.

I urge you to believe in all that makes you unique. Believe in that which makes you brilliant and irreplaceable. Believe in your own Greatness — because that can be the hardest form of Greatness to ask ourselves to see.

Believe in your own perfectly imperfect path. Believe in your own light — even in your darkest moments, it will never forsake you.

Our world desperately needs more dreamers and believers so decide today to believe in all that makes you Great! Yes, there will be falls. Yes, there will be tumbles. Yes, you might even find yourself crushed by a boulder or two... but walk on, even if temporarily, your walking must take place on wheels... even if you can no longer balance the weight of your own body, let your mind stand tall. You are mighty! You are strong!

And nothing, much less a mere boulder, can hold back your GREATNESS!

Yes, dear Global Family, each and every day we live the secret — the secret that it's not in spite of our boulders that we thrive and succeed. It's precisely thanks TO these boulders that we learn just how high we can SOAR!

To Your Greatness and Joy,

xoxo

Meridith

Embrace Your Boulder!

CHAPTER 20

Additional Resources

Web Site: www.iLoveMyImpossible.com

Facebook:

www.facebook.com/schuyisthelimit

www.facebook.com/ilovemyimpossible

Podcast:

www.ilovemyimpossible.com/mypodcasts

Look for the Sky is the Limit Audio Book on Amazon!

The SKY is the LIMIT is also available as a live evening of inspiration. For more information, please check the www.iLoveMyImpossible.com web site or email info@iLoveMyImpossible.com .

Look for the upcoming book by Meridith Hankenson Alexander that features not only the Facebook updates but additional insights, behind the scenes perspectives and inspiration.

Meridith Hankenson Alexander is available for live events and trainings. For more information, please email concierge@iLoveMyImpossible.com

A special thank you to all who took such great photos of Schuy during her adventures, especially the wonderful Brontë Wittpenn who so generously allowed her photo of Schuy in Montana to become the face of our Facebook page!

Thank you so much for coming with us along this journey! If you enjoyed this collection of posts from Schuy is the Limit, please let us know by leaving a review. We wish you a life filled with your own variation of Greatness — whatever that may be. There are no boulders so big that they can diminish your shine. You cannot get this journey wrong. You have got this! You are mighty! Let any scars that you may carry become the brightest jewels in your crown of Life!

In Joy,

Meridith

Made in the USA
Columbia, SC
12 June 2018